MW00465587

Joyce Appleby on *Thomas Jefferson*
Louis Auchincloss on *Theodore Roosevelt*
Jean H. Baker on *James Buchanan*
H. W. Brands on *Woodrow Wilson*
Douglas Brinkley on *Gerald R. Ford*
Josiah Bunting III on *Ulysses S. Grant*
James MacGregor Burns and Susan Dunn on *George Washington*
Charles W. Calhoun on *Benjamin Harrison*
Gail Collins on *William Henry Harrison*
Robert Dallek on *Harry S. Truman*
John W. Dean on *Warren G. Harding*
John Patrick Diggins on *John Adams*
E. L. Doctorow on *Abraham Lincoln*
Elizabeth Drew on *Richard M. Nixon*
Annette Gordon-Reed on *Andrew Johnson*
Henry F. Graff on *Grover Cleveland*
David Greenberg on *Calvin Coolidge*
Gary Hart on *James Monroe*
Hendrik Hertzberg on *Jimmy Carter*
Roy Jenkins on *Franklin Delano Roosevelt*
Zachary Karabell on *Chester Alan Arthur*
Lewis H. Lapham on *William Howard Taft*
William E. Leuchtenburg on *Herbert Hoover*
Timothy Naftali on *George Bush*
Kevin Phillips on *William McKinley*
Robert V. Remini on *John Quincy Adams*
Ira Rutkow on *James A. Garfield*
John Seigenthaler on *James K. Polk*
Hans L. Trefousse on *Rutherford B. Hayes*
Tom Wicker on *Dwight D. Eisenhower*
Ted Widmer on *Martin Van Buren*
Sean Wilentz on *Andrew Jackson*
Garry Wills on *James Madison*

James A. Garfield

Ira Rutkow

James A. Garfield

THE AMERICAN PRESIDENTS

ARTHUR M. SCHLESINGER, JR., GENERAL EDITOR

Times Books

HENRY HOLT AND COMPANY, NEW YORK

Times Books
Henry Holt and Company, LLC
Publishers since 1866
175 Fifth Avenue
New York, New York 10010
www.henryholt.com

Henry Holt® is a registered trademark of
Henry Holt and Company, LLC.

Frontispiece: Portrait of President Garfield © CORBIS

Library of Congress Cataloging-in-Publication Data

Rutkow, Ira M.
    James A. Garfield / Ira Rutkow.—1st ed.
        p.   cm.—(The American presidents series)
    Includes bibliographical references and index.
    ISBN-13: 978-0-8050-6950-1
    ISBN-10: 0-8050-6950-X
        1. Garfield, James A. (James Abram), 1831–1881.   2. Presidents—
United States—Biography.   I. Title.   II. American presidents series
(Times Books (Firm))

E687.R88 2006
973.8'4092—dc22
[B]   2006040415

First Edition 2006

Printed in the United States of America
1   3   5   7   9   10   8   6   4   2

September 18, 1881

President James A. Garfield: *Do you think my name will have a place in history?*

Colonel Almon A. Rockwell: *Yes, a grand one, but a grander one in human hearts. . . . You have a great work yet to perform.*

President James A. Garfield: *No, my work is done.*

—as reported by Robert Reyburn, M.D.,
Journal of the American Medical Association, 1894

Contents

Editor's Note

THE AMERICAN PRESIDENCY

The president is the central player in the American political order. That would seem to contradict the intentions of the Founding Fathers. Remembering the horrid example of the British monarchy, they invented a separation of powers in order, as Justice Brandeis later put it, "to preclude the exercise of arbitrary power." Accordingly, they divided the government into three allegedly equal and coordinate branches—the executive, the legislative, and the judiciary.

But a system based on the tripartite separation of powers has an inherent tendency toward inertia and stalemate. One of the three branches must take the initiative if the system is to move. The executive branch alone is structurally capable of taking that initiative. The Founders must have sensed this when they accepted Alexander Hamilton's proposition in the Seventieth Federalist that "energy in the executive is a leading character in the definition of good government." They thus envisaged a strong president—but within an equally strong system of constitutional accountability. (The term *imperial presidency* arose in the 1970s to describe the situation when the balance between power and accountability is upset in favor of the executive.)

The American system of self-government thus comes to focus in the presidency—"the vital place of action in the system," as Woodrow Wilson put it. Henry Adams, himself the great-grandson and grandson of presidents as well as the most brilliant of American historians, said that the American president "resembles the commander of a ship at sea. He must have a helm to grasp, a course to steer, a port to seek." The men in the White House (thus far only men, alas) in steering their chosen courses have shaped our destiny as a nation.

Biography offers an easy education in American history, rendering the past more human, more vivid, more intimate, more accessible, more connected to ourselves. Biography reminds us that presidents are not supermen. They are human beings too, worrying about decisions, attending to wives and children, juggling balls in the air, and putting on their pants one leg at a time. Indeed, as Emerson contended, "There is properly no history; only biography."

Presidents serve us as inspirations, and they also serve us as warnings. They provide bad examples as well as good. The nation, the Supreme Court has said, has "no right to expect that it will always have wise and humane rulers, sincerely attached to the principles of the Constitution. Wicked men, ambitious of power, with hatred of liberty and contempt of law, may fill the place once occupied by Washington and Lincoln."

The men in the White House express the ideals and the values, the frailties and the flaws, of the voters who send them there. It is altogether natural that we should want to know more about the virtues and the vices of the fellows we have elected to govern us. As we know more about them, we will know more about ourselves. The French political philosopher Joseph de Maistre said, "Every nation has the government it deserves."

At the start of the twenty-first century, forty-two men have made it to the Oval Office. (George W. Bush is counted our forty-third president, because Grover Cleveland, who served nonconsecutive terms, is counted twice.) Of the parade of presidents, a dozen or so lead the polls periodically conducted by historians and political scientists. What makes a great president?

Great presidents possess, or are possessed by, a vision of an ideal America. Their passion, as they grasp the helm, is to set the ship of state on the right course toward the port they seek. Great presidents also have a deep psychic connection with the needs, anxieties, dreams of people. "I do not believe," said Wilson, "that any man can lead who does not act . . . under the impulse of a profound sympathy with those whom he leads—a sympathy which is insight—an insight which is of the heart rather than of the intellect."

"All of our great presidents," said Franklin D. Roosevelt, "were leaders of thought at a time when certain ideas in the life of the nation had to be clarified." So Washington incarnated the idea of federal union, Jefferson and Jackson the idea of democracy, Lincoln union and freedom, Cleveland rugged honesty. Theodore Roosevelt and Wilson, said FDR, were both "moral leaders, each in his own way and his own time, who used the presidency as a pulpit."

To succeed, presidents not only must have a port to seek but they must convince Congress and the electorate that it is a port worth seeking. Politics in a democracy is ultimately an educational process, an adventure in persuasion and consent. Every president stands in Theodore Roosevelt's bully pulpit.

The greatest presidents in the scholars' rankings, Washington, Lincoln, and Franklin Roosevelt, were leaders who confronted and overcame the republic's greatest crises. Crisis widens presidential opportunities for bold and imaginative action. But it does not guarantee presidential greatness. The crisis of secession did not spur Buchanan or the crisis of depression spur Hoover to creative leadership. Their inadequacies in the face of crisis allowed Lincoln and the second Roosevelt to show the difference individuals make to history. Still, even in the absence of first-order crisis, forceful and persuasive presidents—Jefferson, Jackson, James K. Polk, Theodore Roosevelt, Harry Truman, John F. Kennedy, Ronald Reagan, George W. Bush—are able to impose their own priorities on the country.

The diverse drama of the presidency offers a fascinating set of tales. Biographies of American presidents constitute a chronicle of wisdom and folly, nobility and pettiness, courage and cunning, forthrightness and deceit, quarrel and consensus. The turmoil perennially swirling around the White House illuminates the heart of the American democracy.

It is the aim of the American Presidents series to present the grand panorama of our chief executives in volumes compact enough for the busy reader, lucid enough for the student, authoritative enough for the scholar. Each volume offers a distillation of character and career. I hope that these lives will give readers some understanding of the pitfalls and potentialities of the presidency and also of the responsibilities of citizenship. Truman's famous sign—"The buck stops here"—tells only half the story. Citizens cannot escape the ultimate responsibility. It is in the voting booth, not on the presidential desk, that the buck finally stops.

—Arthur M. Schlesinger, Jr.

James A. Garfield

1

Early Years

Saturday, July 2, 1881, was as pleasant a day as can come with an American summer weekend. For James Abram Garfield, the twentieth president of the United States, the exquisite weather heightened his anticipation of an enjoyable train ride to Williamstown, Massachusetts. He planned to attend the commencement of his alma mater, Williams College, and then, with his wife, Lucretia, take an extended trip through New England. For the forty-nine-year-old Garfield, it had been a stressful four months since his inauguration; he was in the midst of a bitter fight between the warring Stalwart and Half-Breed factions of his Republican Party over political patronage. The new president looked forward to a relaxing getaway.

Garfield had been awake since early morning and, after some horseplay with his sons, awaited the arrival of James G. Blaine, his secretary of state. Eighteen years had passed since their simultaneous swearings in as United States congressmen, and, although their relationship had been stormy at times, they were now close friends. Garfield wanted one more opportunity to talk politics, especially about his growing disfavor for Vice President Chester A. Arthur, who had taken positions in opposition to him on some of the more contentious issues before Congress. Blaine accompanied Garfield on the five-minute carriage ride to the Baltimore and Potomac train depot. Despite the assassination of Abraham Lincoln sixteen years earlier, the American president still had no personal bodyguards. Newspaper editors thought nothing of publicly posting his daily schedule, including details such as the location and time of departure for meetings and even vacations.

At 9:20 A.M., Garfield and Blaine, walking side by side, entered the station's ladies' waiting room—men were also allowed in the area. Several individuals milled about, including a slightly built, shabbily dressed man who paced up and down rather nervously. As the president and secretary of state passed through the room, the odd-looking stranger spotted them and suddenly whirled toward the two men. Positioning himself six feet behind and to the right of Garfield, the man drew an ivory-handled revolver from his pocket, leveled it at the president, and fired twice. The first shot caused a slight flesh wound of the right arm but the second entered the middle of the right side of Garfield's back, jolting him forward. The president's legs broke from under him as he slumped to the wooden floor. Blaine, with a terrified look, cried out, "My God, he has been murdered! What is the meaning of this?"[1] Turning toward the shooter, he recognized him as Charles J. Guiteau, a persistent job seeker, who for months had pestered State Department and White House officials regarding patronage positions. Guiteau attempted to flee the scene but was apprehended by a policeman. As the assassin was dragged away, he told the officer, "I did it and will go to jail for it. I am a Stalwart and Arthur will be president."[2]

Onlookers gathered around the fallen president as messengers were dispatched to look for any available physician. Within five minutes, a health officer for the District of Columbia arrived. He found Garfield stuporous, with large beads of perspiration upon his brow. As a method of stimulation—and in keeping with contemporary medical practice—the doctor had Garfield swallow a mixture of brandy and aromatic ammonia spirit. With Garfield more alert, he was turned on his side and his coat lifted to reveal the wound with its slight hemorrhage. Garfield inquired about the injury and, when told it was not serious, shook his head and said, "Doctor, I am a dead man."[3] He asked to be taken back to the White House. As the horse-drawn ambulance clattered over the rough cobblestones of Sixth Street, the injured Garfield was jostled to and fro. A surging crowd struggled to keep up with the fast-moving wagon. Brought to the family room at the White House, Garfield received round-the-clock medical care, but despite extraordinary efforts his end came in a tortuous and controversial death seventy-nine days later, on September 19.

James A. Garfield soon disappeared from the public's memory, and he remains one of America's least remembered chief executives. "For who was Garfield, martyred man, and who had seen him in the streets of life?" asked the novelist Thomas Wolfe. "Who could believe that his footfalls ever sounded on a lonely pavement?"[4] But Garfield did exist—he was a son, a husband, and a father. He lived and breathed and laughed and cried and played a major role in American politics. He was the last of the nation's "born in a log cabin" presidents, a general during the Civil War, and the quintessential rags-to-riches, self-made American man. Even in death, Garfield came to embody the strive-and-succeed spirit that marked the country's socioeconomic climate as the nineteenth century came to a close. The clinical reasons for why he died—physician incompetence mixed with an all-consuming medical hubris—provided a momentum within the medical profession that helped change the course of American health care.

Garfield was president during the Gilded Age, so named by Mark Twain in an 1873 utopian satire. Twain's title was not a laudatory label but a triple play on words. There was the gilt of the upper class's overindulgences, the guilt brought on by the financial shenanigans of Wall Street tycoons and robber barons, and the guilds that represented special interest groups, labor unions, political bosses, and even the manufacturing monopolies. The country paid more attention to the outsize personalities of industrialists such as Andrew Carnegie, Henry Clay Frick, Jay Gould, J. P. Morgan, and John D. Rockefeller than to the activities of career politicians who could not be differentiated by actions or appearances. Indeed, the federal government had moved away from the extensive national attention that it had received through the Civil War and the early years of Reconstruction.

Although the so-called lost presidents of the Gilded Age (Rutherford B. Hayes, James A. Garfield, Chester A. Arthur, Grover Cleveland, and Benjamin Harrison) are embedded only in our historical unconscious, they were an essential element in the tapestry of American life. These men might not have had starring roles in the eyes of the public, but their actions had consequences that affected the lives of millions of Americans. For this reason alone, a recounting of the career of James A. Garfield, the "young-man-in-a-hurry," the "political animal," the short-lived president of the United States, is fitting.

The Western Reserve was a poorly populated, fertile wilderness of old-growth forests when James Abram Garfield was born in the little frontier village of Orange, a few miles south of Cleveland, on November 19, 1831. Recalling his birth, his mother said, "James A. was the largest Babe I ever had, he looked like a red Irishman."[5] Like many of the area's settlers, successive generations of Garfield's ancestors had wended their way from New England, through the valleys of upstate New York and Pennsylvania, to end up west of the Alleghenies in northern Ohio. The Garfield family had never flourished in a financial sense, and life on their twenty-acre farm with its tiny log cabin became even more difficult when Abram Garfield, the father of James and his three older siblings, died from a pneumonia-like illness in 1833. Eliza Garfield, the mother, was a woman of considerable pluck and religiosity who managed to maintain the farm's viability while raising her children by herself. "Anything that approached impurity of life and speech, in any degree, was hateful to her beyond expression," remarked an early Garfield biographer. "In that household there was a sort of flaming sword swinging constantly against all forms of indecency and immorality."[6] James was clearly her favorite and he maintained a close relationship with his mother throughout his life.

Of the many stories (and legends) that surround Garfield's early years, the one constant is that of a kindhearted youngster who was a quick learner, but restless and inclined to approach few activities with a serious manner. Although physically strapping, Garfield was awkward and lacked all manner of manual dexterity. "To learn the use of an ax," wrote his wife years later, "he was obliged almost a score of times to be shut up in the house or hobble on crutches, disabled by fearful gashes made through his carelessness."[7] Garfield family lore long told of how young James nearly killed his cousin, Silas Boynton, by a misplaced ax blow. As he matured, there was a likable frontier independence to Garfield's personality that manifested itself in two telling and overarching character traits: a determination that each chapter of his life's work would positively and unfailingly lead to a next phase (i.e., he was ambitious and disciplined); and a need to show no fear toward any mental or physical challenge (i.e., he was intelligent and manly).

These qualities were already evident when, at sixteen, Garfield left home to build a life different from that of a simple backwoods farmer. Despite his minimal formal education he had become a voracious reader, and a series of nautical novels had filled him with a teenage fantasy of becoming a sailor. His mother was aghast and bitterly opposed to her son's leaving. But the determined Garfield was not to be dissuaded and he proceeded to tramp through the Reserve to Cleveland's Lake Erie waterfront.

This was the era of the American canal; waterways crisscrossed the countryside, connecting the Great Lakes with the growing industrial towns in the Northeast. Iron and copper ore arrived from the west by schooner and were loaded on canal barges where the raw stone was moved to the manufacturing centers. The canals themselves were primitive earthen fabrications, filled with mud, teeming with mosquitoes, and requiring rigged teams of horses or mules on a bordering towpath to move the barge along. It was a laborious affair and provided little in the way of the "seamanship" that Garfield hoped to acquire. For several months, he served alternately as a bowsman, deckhand, and steerman, but his prowess in handling the haul was not matched by an ability to swim. By Garfield's own account, he fell into the water fourteen times and often came close to drowning. Garfield's canal experiment came to an end in early October 1848. Between the ever-present canal ruffians, the near drownings, the physical toll of hard labor, and the sudden onset of a high fever—one of the symptoms of malaria—the young man called it quits and headed home.

Thoughts of a seafaring life were put aside as a more introspective son returned to his mother's nursing and urgings. She considered education a priority and importuned him to resume his schooling. With seventeen of his mother's dollars in his pocket, the teenager set off for Geauga Academy in nearby Chester. In Garfield's words, "No greener boy ever started out to school."[8] Humility aside, a ready capacity to adjust to new circumstances always marked Garfield's life. In a year and a half at Geauga, he picked up the rudiments of grammar, mathematics, and philosophy. He enjoyed writing and started a diary (his daily musings would continue for the next three decades), but it was the study of elocution and ancient and modern languages that held his greatest interest. Garfield joined the debate society, where he began to understand the power of the speaker's platform. "It creates some excitement," he wrote. "I love agitation and investigation and glory in defending unpopular truth against popular error."[9]

In the autumn of 1851, Garfield matriculated at Western Reserve Eclectic Institute at Hiram. It was typical of the region's "colleges." Poorly staffed, without a dollar of endowment, and with only one redbrick scholastic building, its main merit was that it allowed ambitious students to study at their own accelerated pace. Garfield attacked the rigidly classical curriculum with a profound zest for learning and Hiram became his second home. Indeed, the school would long claim Garfield's loyalty and he would return to its campus, as a steadfast alumnus, throughout his adulthood.

Garfield rose at four or five in the morning, attended classes for ten hours a day, read Demosthenes, Herodotus, Homer, Livy, and

Tacitus, mastered Greek and Latin, managed to learn geometry on his own, and often stayed up until midnight, ensuring that his carrel's candle was the last to be extinguished. "He had a wide-awake curiosity which seemed never to be satiated," wrote a fellow student. "A new thing, however unimportant, always attracted his attention."[10] His diary jottings became more literate and, as at Geauga, Garfield's most enjoyable intellectual outlet was debating. He became known as a formidable public speaker and participated in *lyceums*—as such debates were called—not only at Hiram but throughout the Reserve. So exceptional were his oratorical and scholarly skills that Garfield was asked to deliver the valedictory address at the conclusion of his first term. During his second and third years at Hiram, he was recruited to teach a variety of lower-level courses to the younger students.

Despite his flair for the spoken word and his ability to stir an audience, Garfield's years at Hiram brought no evident interest in politics. "Politics are now raging with great violence," he wrote in the midst of the 1852 presidential campaign. "I am profoundly ignorant of its multifarious phases, and am not inclined to study it. I am exceedingly disgusted with the wire pulling of politicians and the total disregard for truth in all their operations."[11] Such disinterest was about to change as Garfield sought to broaden his cultural and educational background. The Eclectic Institute did not have state authority to confer a college degree—it would not become Hiram College until 1867—and Garfield looked eastward for a baccalaureate.

Williams College, in the extreme northwest corner of Massachusetts, was administered by Mark Hopkins, a compelling and energetic educator. One of the most able and successful of nineteenth-century American college presidents, Hopkins was an ordained Congregational minister who would have a profound influence on Garfield's life. At Williams, under Hopkins's guidance, a distinguished faculty had been hired, libraries containing 25,000 books were built, and a reputation for thorough and demanding scholarship was earned. In September 1854, Garfield was admitted to the school's junior class, having received credit for two years of college-level studies at Hiram.

Williams's third-year academic program included astronomy, chemistry, German, Greek, Latin, mechanics, and political economy, and the depth of its extracurricular offerings was exceptional. As at Geauga and Hiram, Garfield's spoken eloquence and remarkable academic prowess soon set him apart from other students. Standing out with his large physique, luxuriant chestnut whiskers, and self-confident manner, Garfield's quick repartee prompted a classmate to label him "undoubtedly one of the greatest natural debaters ever seen at Williams."[12] Even Hopkins was said to convulse with laughter, his legs described as twisted into a knot, as he listened to Garfield's ingratiating humor and biting sarcasm. At the end of his first fall term, the well-liked Garfield, who was always in need of extra income, was invited to spend several weeks teaching penmanship to the schoolchildren in the nearby town of Pownal, Vermont. In a curious coincidence of history, Garfield occupied a position that had been filled the previous year by Chester A. Arthur, his future vice presidential running mate.

By January 1855, Garfield had clearly become one of Hopkins's favorites. "There was a large general capacity applicable to any subject," reminisced Hopkins about Garfield's student days. "There was no pretence of genius, or alternation of spasmodic effort, but a satisfactory accomplishment in all directions."[13] Garfield, in turn, was impressed by Hopkins's intellectual abilities. "There is a symmetry about his mind that is admirable," he wrote in his diary. "I think he is a great man."[14] Garfield took Hopkins's courses on religious and philosophical matters and, despite being unaccustomed to the educator's critical style of thinking, began to utilize this manner of reasoning and apply it to a wide range of scholarly activities. From literature to metaphysics, Garfield became a respected campus scholar.

Equally as important as this newfound intellect, Hopkins and the Williams experience began to turn Garfield's interests toward politics. "I have been instructed tonight on the political condition of our country," Garfield wrote in his diary, "and from this time forward I shall hope to know more about its movements and interests."[15] He embraced the abolitionist movement, attended the antislavery lectures of Henry Ward Beecher, and satirized the Know-Nothing Party in a political poem. Discussions about the great political events of the era—the status of Kansas, the dangers of foreign immigrants, the influence of the Roman Catholic Church, the justice of the Crimean War, the desirability of an elected judiciary branch of government, and the constitutionality of several personal liberty laws—found their way into Garfield's daily ruminations. In the spring of his senior year, he attended a political meeting in support of the new Republican Party and its presidential candidate, John C. Frémont, at which he gave his first political stump speech. Garfield even mentioned that he considered "women wronged socially and intellectually by the usages of society."[16]

On commencement day in August 1856, twenty-four-year-old James Garfield, chief editor of the *Williams Quarterly* (the literary magazine), president of the Philologian Society (the literary club), member of the Theological Society, leader of the campus anti-secret society, spokesperson for the school's anti-fraternity faction, and class salutatorian, gave the day's "Metaphysical Oration." It was among the top academic honors a Williams graduate could receive. Hopkins, sitting in a high pulpit, leaned forward and listened as Garfield took command of the audience. According to one eyewitness, "pride and affection he might have felt for a son" filled Hopkins's eyes.[17] At the conclusion, applause rocked the church and thrown bouquets littered the floor as a confident Garfield ended his college career.

For the budding politician, the Williams College experience was the most important of all his formal educational endeavors. In Williamstown, Garfield learned the art of getting along with all personality types. He grew to respect individuals of different social backgrounds and political persuasions. Williams "broke down the sectarian narrowness which had come to threaten his future development," wrote one Garfield biographer.[18] Equally important, the backwoods Garfield was accepted and respected by Williams's more closed-minded, socially conscious East Coast students. In short, Garfield had an extensive and positive first experience with the world outside the Western Reserve of Ohio. And, as would be true in every stage of his life—parlaying one chapter into the next—Garfield's Williams days established an important foundation for his next undertaking.

Indeed, in later years, Garfield's early life would be considered among his chief political strengths. The tale of the poor farmboy who rose out of the wilds of northern Ohio to the White House would come to personify the American dream of the self-made man—especially so when Horatio Alger, Jr., the writer of boys' stories, extolled Garfield's rise in an 1881 biography, aptly titled *From Canal Boy to President*. Preachers and politicians would exhort the nation's youth to follow Garfield's examples of diligent study and hard work to overcome all forms of adversity. Even Garfield himself would not be above exploiting his childhood privations for political profit. But as he returned to Ohio in 1856, there truly seemed no limit to what Garfield could accomplish. One of his uncles was already telling family members that James would be president one day.

In Ohio's interior in the 1850s, it was considered a great personal achievement to have graduated from a sophisticated eastern college. As a result, Garfield, who came back to teach ancient languages and literature at the Western Reserve Eclectic Institute, was received as a man of distinction and substance. However, as much as Garfield was a changed person, the Eclectic, with its single, ugly, redbrick building, remained academically and administratively backward. It is a credit to Garfield's ambition and determination that, in spite of his disappointment with the Eclectic's unchanged ways, he demonstrated his usual zeal in his roles as a respected teacher and sought-after public speaker. Successes followed one another and, within a year of his return, Garfield was asked to assume the presidency of the institution. He gladly accepted but grew increasingly uncertain about his future plans. "You and I know that teaching is not the work in which a man can live and grow," he complained to a boyhood friend. "I am succeeding in the school here better than I had any reason to hope, but yet my heart will never be satisfied to spend my life in teaching."[19]

Soon afterward, Garfield decided to draw on his growing prominence as a stepping-stone to a new life—in politics. These were the early days of the Republican Party, when bloody battles between pro- and antislavery forces in Kansas dominated the nation's political headlines. Garfield, an ardent antislavery man, became known as an effective Republican Party spokesperson, and his reward for his service was election, in 1859, as the youngest member of the Ohio senate. Garfield had proved an enthusiastic campaigner and delivered over thirty speeches at a time in American politics when such talks were verbal marathons, averaging two hours apiece. "The young Senator—for he is not yet thirty—stepped at once from comparative obscurity into genuine popularity as a political speaker," wrote a reporter for the Cincinnati *Commercial*. "From this time . . . his party will demand his services on the stump."[20]

Three qualities immediately set Garfield apart from other senators: a prodigious capacity to grasp the minutiae of legislation, extraordinary speechmaking abilities, and a genuineness in forming friendships. He drafted a statistics-filled committee report concerning a geological survey to determine the natural resources of Ohio, another on the education of abandoned and pauper children, and a third detailing the regulation of weights and measures through a comparison of the English and American systems. As the keynote speaker at a lavish banquet in Louisville in honor of the Kentucky and Tennessee legislatures, Garfield's oratorical skills were used to persuade members of the two governing bodies to accept an invitation to visit Ohio. The idea, backed by Ohio's governor, was an attempt to lessen sectional differences and squelch the clamor concerning secession. Garfield made an impassioned plea for maintenance of the Union. "No note of disunion shall be heard," he proclaimed, while asking that the West (today's Midwest) remain a symbol of the indivisible unity of the country.[21] The legislators accepted the invitation and their trip through Ohio became a celebration of goodwill.

The success of Garfield's mission to Louisville attracted attention from Ohio's newspapers and senior Republican Party leaders. "He had that simple, affectionate way, which charms people," noted William Dean Howells, a young newspaper correspondent for the *Ohio State Journal*.[22] Salmon P. Chase, a former Ohio governor and U.S. senator, and a leading national figure within the party, took an instant liking to Garfield. With Chase's backing, Garfield was recruited to canvass the state giving speeches for the 1860 Republican national ticket. "Voted for Lincoln and Hamlin," Garfield wrote in his diary on election night. "God be praised!!"[23]

In the short span of two years, Garfield had become one of Ohio's more prominent politicians. In addition, his life was changing in other ways. In November 1858, he married his childhood sweetheart, Lucretia "Crete" Rudolph, a shy, dark-eyed brunette. They had known each other since sharing classrooms at Geauga Academy and the Eclectic. The Garfields rented a little cottage in Hiram fronting their old college campus, where he continued his duties as president of the institute. Under his leadership, the institute prospered. The number of students rose to new levels and the school managed to remain financially solvent. A year and a half later, Garfield became a father. Looking to further his political career, he was admitted to the Ohio bar, under the contemporary practice of independently reading a number of respected law books and then presenting himself for examination. Despite his familial commitments and the commencement of a legal practice, Garfield remained characteristically restless. "When I am sitting," he grumbled to Crete, "I long to be walking and when I am walking I long to be sitting."[24]

By the time of Garfield's second Ohio senate session in January 1861, the secession of South Carolina had brought disunion closer to reality. The previously conciliatory Garfield, who had traveled to Louisville only a few months before to woo his neighboring states' legislators, returned to Columbus a full-blown hawk. Sectional compromise was no longer possible in his mind. What caused this shift in his attitude remains historical conjecture. "I do not see any way, outside a miracle of God, which can avoid civil war, with all its attendant horrors," Garfield wrote to a friend. "Peaceable dissolution is utterly impossible. . . . All that is left us is to arm and prepare to defend ourselves and the Federal Government."[25] An internecine struggle was about to engulf the nation, and Garfield, in a characteristic manner, would make certain that he had a leadership role in the conflict.

2

The Civil War

In April 1861, South Carolina's Fort Sumter was shelled. Garfield, who had grown impatient with Southern political demands, welcomed news of the fort's fall. "I am glad we are defeated at Sumter," he wrote to a friend. "It will rouse the people."[1] War fever gripped Ohio, and Garfield, who was against any hint of political compromise, strongly supported the federal government's authority to begin legal proceedings against the seceding states. He had previously introduced a bill to make treason against the United States punishable by life imprisonment. Garfield voted against a proposed Thirteenth Amendment that would have forbidden Congress from ever legislating on the subject of slavery and defended the state's right to appropriate a million dollars for military expenses, including the outfitting of a 6,000-man militia. And when President Abraham Lincoln issued a call for 75,000 Northern troops to serve for three months, Garfield, in an act of political grandstanding, asked that Ohio alone furnish 20,000 soldiers and three million dollars. Garfield anticipated a relatively short but bloody war, and he began to familiarize himself with various military treatises and studied the campaigns of Napoleon and Wellington.

Garfield considered his personal and political attainments to have earned him a position as an officer in the Union army. Friends expressed the flattering, but unrealistic, opinion that he deserved a brigadier generalship. The impact of rank and combat experience was not lost on Garfield. Military leaders commanded respect and often left the armed services to assume high political office. Certainly, the military exploits of Presidents George Washington, James Monroe, Andrew Jackson, William Henry Harrison, Zachary Taylor, and Franklin Pierce loomed large in Garfield's thinking. However, an editorial in the anti-Republican *Weekly Portage Sentinel* attacked Garfield as lacking military education and experience. His sole goal, according to the writer, was an overwhelming political ambition "to leap from the walks of a private citizen to the position of a military chieftain."[2]

Despite such criticism, Garfield realized that future political opportunities might depend on his demonstration of leadership in a combat zone. Offering his services to the Ohio governor, Garfield was commissioned a lieutenant colonel. He was subsequently promoted to colonel of the 42nd Ohio Volunteers, a regiment that Garfield recruited largely from among his former students at the Eclectic Institute. Garfield's military ascension followed the well-established American tradition whereby a prominent businessman or a politically influential person would, under a governor's authority, recruit a fighting force and, in return, be named the unit's commander. In December 1861, after four months of drilling, the 42nd Ohio and its ambitious commander were ordered to Louisville.

The United States Army was faced with a minor but annoying problem in the Big Sandy Valley on the eastern Kentucky side of the rugged Cumberland Mountains. Confederate troops had invaded from Virginia and were attempting to recruit the local populace. Garfield was charged with driving the rebels out. In later years, the Sandy Valley campaign and its daylong Battle of Middle Creek, with three Union dead and eighteen wounded and two dozen Confederate casualties, would be regarded as a minor affair having no substantive bearing on the outcome of the war. But, in the winter of 1862, Garfield's victory and the eventual withdrawal of Confederate troops brought him much celebrity. His commanding officer observed that Garfield's actions represented "the highest qualities of a soldier—fortitude, perseverance, and courage."[3] Tales were told of Garfield's derring-do: when a rise in the Sandy Valley River made it difficult for the steamer pilots to conduct their vessels as food supplies ran low, a confident Garfield, relying on the experience of his boyhood canal days, brought a ship through in safety. Newspapers sang his praises—a front-page headline in the *New York Times* even mentioned his name—and America had a genuine war hero. Of course, the ever deliberate Garfield also contributed to the public relations windfall by issuing a widely praised but self-aggrandizing proclamation to the people of Sandy Valley. "I have come among you to restore the honor of the Union," he wrote, "and to bring back the old banner which you once loved, but which, by the machinations of evil men, and by mutual misunderstanding, has been dishonored."[4] Back in Ohio, Garfield's supporters lobbied an already sympathetic governor, hoping that their hero's deeds entitled him to a battlefield promotion. The governor agreed and, in March, Garfield's advancement to brigadier general garnered considerable press attention. For the remainder of his life, regardless of his political achievements, he would always be best known as General Garfield.

Despite his generalcy, Garfield began to fear that with the war dragging on he would be regarded as simply one of a growing number of state-appointed brigade commanders. This was a discouraging thought for someone with national political ambitions, especially since he had received encouraging letters from his constituents urging him to run for Congress. With his health in serious decline—Garfield was ill with dysentery, hemorrhoids, and a hepatitis-induced jaundice—and increasingly frustrated over the military's and government's inept prosecution of the war, he wrote to one of his hometown political mentors about his future ambitions. "It seems to me that the successful ending of the war is the smaller of the two tasks imposed upon the government," remarked Garfield. "There will spring up out of this war a score of new questions and new dangers. The settlement of these will be of even more vital importance than the ending of the war. I do not hesitate to tell you that I believe I could do some service in Congress in that work and I should prefer that to continuing in the army."[5]

Returning home on a medical furlough, Garfield realized that with the prevailing "lame duck" system, the Congress to be elected in November 1862 would not assemble in Washington in regular session until December 1863. Appreciating that once his health returned he could resume his military command, albeit with the added prestige and power of a congressman-elect, there was little to dissuade Garfield from seeking the nomination. The Nineteenth District consisted of a new grouping of five counties, and the political gossip focused on Garfield, the well-known educator, lawyer, politician, and military leader. Despite the talk, he played coy with the nominating process. "If the people of the District want me I take it that it is their business to tell me so and not mine to coax them to have me," he wrote his mother.[6] Such nonchalance typified what became Garfield's attitude toward seeking national political office. For the remainder of his life, including his presidential election, he considered it unseemly if his personal ambitions appeared to conflict with the spontaneous will of the people. Indeed, in this, his first run for higher office, Garfield did not even attend the nominating convention. His absence probably mattered little since a group of devoted supporters—knowing that he endorsed all their actions—labored intensively on his behalf. In early September 1862, the Republican nomination was secured. In view of the district's Republican leanings, everyone knew the nomination amounted to election to the House of Representatives.

With his health restored and kudos surrounding his nomination, Garfield received orders from Secretary of War Edwin Stanton directing him to report to Washington to discuss plans for the resumption of his military duties. A few days after his arrival, Garfield was befriended by the aristocratic and powerful Secretary of the Treasury Salmon P. Chase, who asked him to be his houseguest. It was a flattering invitation, especially because Chase's home served as the social center of the Republican administration. Chase, a solemn and dignified individual who would later be named chief justice of the United States, was impressed by Garfield's intelligence and ambition to become part of the Republican leadership. Chase saw in the thirty-one-year-old Garfield a younger version of himself, a self-made individual whose career path from laborer to educator to politician paralleled his own. Chase's discussions about the mysteries of government finance encouraged Garfield's interest in the sometimes arcane subject that would shortly become a chief concentration of his own public career. The strong-willed and egocentric Chase proved a perfect mentor and, for four months, Garfield thrived in an atmosphere where he was offered endless opportunities to meet the nation's mighty. They became close friends—Chase, a lonely widower, never had a son and Garfield never knew his father—and Garfield would later espouse many of Chase's causes. "Chase is," wrote Garfield, "by far the strongest man in the administration and he seems to be thoroughly imbued with a moral and religious sense of the duties of the government in relation to the war."[7]

In November, Garfield defeated his Democratic opponent for Congress by a two-to-one margin, running well ahead of the national and state Republican ticket as a whole. The four months in Washington might have added little to his military credentials, but the time proved invaluable for his political future. Garfield was a philosophically transformed congressman-to-be. Like Chase, he now considered himself part of the radical wing of the Republican Party. He was particularly partisan in his hostility to Northern Democrats, whom he viewed as too soft on the rebellious political leaders and populace of the South. As a war hawk, Garfield had misgivings about Lincoln's apparent timidity in prosecuting the military aspects of the war. "I think we are passing through a most fearful time," Garfield wrote to a friend back home in Ohio. "The most fearful aspect by far is the painful weakness and uncertainty of the Administration. I have no words to tell you how sad my heart is over it all."[8] Garfield believed that combat efforts would never succeed unless more resolute antislavery men assumed greater military and political authority.

In December 1862, Union forces suffered a humiliating defeat at Fredericksburg, Virginia. For Garfield, this embarrassing rout added to his desire to reenter active military life, in expectation of personally affecting the course of the war. "I hope the country is awaking to the truth of the doctrine I have tried to preach to them for the last six months," Garfield wrote to one of his political strategists. "There is no hope of the Republic unless we pulverize the great rebel armies."[9] Garfield wished to be promoted to major general with an independent brigade command or some other high-ranking position with decision-making authority. To prepare for this possibility, he began to write a treatise on the military successes of Frederick the Great of Prussia. The book was never completed because, in January 1863, Garfield was ordered to report to Major General William S. Rosecrans, commander of the newly organized Army of the Cumberland in Murfreesboro, Tennessee.

Rosecrans—"Old Rosy" to his men—was at the height of his fame as a Union combat officer. He had gained immense popularity, especially among his troops, with his fearless assault at Stone River and the subsequent occupation of Murfreesboro. In contrast with the series of Union losses in the east, Rosecrans appeared to have the Confederates on the run. It was Rosecrans's aggressiveness and military sense that most appealed to Garfield. And, since Rosecrans was looking for both a chief of staff and several brigade commanders, it seemed a perfect match. Rosecrans, knowing of Garfield's growing influence and political friendship with Chase, thought it might be useful to have such a person as part of his combat team. First, though, Rosecrans had to be assured of Garfield's loyalty before offering him a high-ranking assignment. Some members of Rosecrans's staff feared that Garfield would act as little more than an in-house spy for Washington's radical Republicans. Thus, Garfield and Rosecrans spent several weeks getting to know each other. "For ten nights I have not gone to bed once before 2:30 o'clock in the morning, frequently not till four," Garfield told a friend. "After one o'clock the General and I have given ourselves up to the discussion of religion, literature and war."[10] As a result of these nighttime discussions, a reassured Rosecrans gave Garfield a choice between commanding a division of several thousand men or serving as his chief of staff.

Garfield was in a quandary. He desired battlefield glory, but Rosecrans's description of the chief of staff position as a kind of alter ego, privy to all major combat decisions, was tempting. Garfield still had misgivings, particularly whether it was prudent to risk his own career on the achievements of one general. "By taking that position," he wrote, "I should make a large investment in Gen. Rosecrans and will it be wise to risk so much stock in that market?"[11] However, holding Rosecrans to his word, that the chief of staff position would be likened to that of a commanding field general, shaping the Army of the Cumberland's policies and strategies, and knowing that he had less than ten months left before Congress convened, Garfield accepted.

Garfield had strong opinions about how the war should be fought; first among these was the need to strike boldly against rebel forces. Initially, Rosecrans fulfilled most of Garfield's expectations. Union forces outflanked the Confederates at Shelbyville and Tullahoma and then regained the whole of middle Tennessee. It was an auspicious start to what Garfield thought would be a decisive strike deep into the heart of Southern territory. With the rebels scattered, he waited for the final offensive to begin. But then Rosecrans suddenly hesitated and began to argue with Secretary Stanton over battlefield strategy and the need for additional troops and equipment. Stanton had a personal dislike for the West Point–educated Rosecrans and the spat degenerated into a series of sarcastic dispatches that resulted in further procrastination. Garfield disagreed with the delay and implored Rosecrans not to dawdle and instead to force an engagement. "I have no words to tell you with," he wrote his wife, "how restive and unsatisfied a spirit I waited and pleaded for striking a sturdy blow."[12]

Whatever influence Garfield had with Rosecrans was on the wane. Growing restless and knowing that he had only a few months left to make his military mark, Garfield took out his frustration in

July in a lengthy letter to Chase. "Thus far," he wrote in describing his disappointment, "the General has been singularly disinclined to grasp the situation with a strong hand and make the advantage his own. . . . Officially I share his counsels and responsibilities even more than I desire; but I beg you to know that this delay is against my judgment and my every wish."[13] Garfield went on to discuss the necessity for an immediate offensive as the only means to prevent auxiliary rebel troops from reinforcing those already dispersed throughout the countryside.

Garfield's letter created quite a stir when its contents became known in Washington. Not only was the missive said to have contributed to the dismissal of Rosecrans later that fall as commander of the Army of the Cumberland, but Garfield's political foes cited it as an example of his underhanded ways. Seventeen years later, his critics would use the letter's contents in a smear campaign during Garfield's presidential bid. Chase showed the letter to Stanton who, in turn, passed it around to other members of the cabinet. As a result, a Washington-based anti-Rosecrans faction surfaced, and it became increasingly difficult for Rosecrans to lead his army at the very time he was being urged to speed up its maneuvering. Stanton, however, was already frustrated with Rosecrans's inaction and the letter did little more than strengthen preexisting prejudices. In all likelihood, Rosecrans would have been dismissed in the coming months even if Garfield had remained silent.

As to Garfield's critics' cries of treachery, Rosecrans was well aware of Garfield's views and that his chief of staff often wrote to Chase about army affairs. Indeed, the Chase-Garfield friendship had probably influenced Rosecrans to offer Garfield the chief of staff position in the first place. Given Garfield's strong views about how the war should be prosecuted, how could he have remained silent if he thought that Rosecrans's inactivity was truly prolonging the war? Garfield can certainly be accused of lacking common sense and not fully appreciating the ethical dilemma of his role as both an army commander's chief of staff and a cabinet officer's friend. Probably in consideration of his political future, Garfield wanted to separate himself from any of Rosecrans's misdeeds and, at the same time, believed he was performing a patriotic albeit anguish-filled act. Rosecrans, despite Garfield's disagreements with him, continued to gratefully acknowledge the work of his chief of staff. "All of my staff merited my warm approbation for ability, zeal, and devotion to duty," Rosecrans stated in his official report of the Tullahoma campaign, "but I am sure they will not consider it invidious if I especially mention Brigadier-General Garfield, ever active, prudent and sagacious. I feel much indebted to him for both counsel and assistance in the administration of this army. He possesses the energy and the instinct of a great commander."[14]

By September 1863, the Army of the Cumberland was again on the move. But Rosecrans was faced with a far more serious situation than he anticipated. Moving into unfamiliar territory on the Tennessee/Georgia border, his supply lines were overextended and elements of his army were more separated than in the past. Communication between divisions was poor, Rosecrans had lost track of the enemy, and the Army of the Cumberland was now needlessly exposed. Garfield was aware of the seriousness of the situation. "A battle is imminent," he told a friend. "I believe the enemy intends now to fight us. He has a large force and the advantage of position. Unless we can outmaneuver him we shall be in a perilous situation."[15] The Battle of Chickamauga thundered for two terrible days. During the first twenty-four hours, there was little change in either army's position, but on the second day the Confederates broke through a gap in the Union troops and routed the Yankees.

From the first cannon blast until after the rebels won their victory, Garfield worked tirelessly at Rosecrans's side. When the Southern forces split the Northern line, one of Rosecrans's divisions was left asunder. Garfield undertook a dangerous ride through enemy lines to ascertain the situation. Whether he went on his own or was ordered by Rosecrans remains historical conjecture, but he reached the front unscathed, although his orderly was killed and his own horse wounded. Garfield found that the division was resolutely holding its position, although it would soon be forced to abandon its location and fall back toward Chattanooga. Garfield's ride—reporters from the *New York Herald* and the *Cincinnati Gazette* were eyewitnesses to his exploits—was widely publicized and in later years became part of the Garfield political legend. For now, the Union's defeat demoralized Rosecrans, brought about further rumormongering from his enemies, and led Lincoln to relieve Rosecrans of his command.

Garfield's departure from Chattanooga marked the end of his military career. Rosecrans issued a general order praising his chief of staff for "invaluable assistance . . . by wise councils and assiduous labors, as well as for his gallantry, good judgment and efficiency."[16] In late October, Garfield arrived in Washington where he delivered his report of the combat operations in Tennessee and received the long-awaited promotion to major general. Garfield was immediately embraced by Chase and his other Washington friends as a triumphant war hero. He was asked to deliver political speeches and participate in Republican political events, but he had doubts about resigning his military commission, especially in view of his new promotion. Not knowing what to do, Garfield met with Lincoln, who told him that he needed men with military experience in Congress to assist him in establishing a more vigorous army. "The President told me he dared not risk a single vote in the House," Garfield wrote to his college mentor, Mark Hopkins. "I did not feel it right to consult my own preference in such a case."[17] Impressed by Lincoln's sincerity and his promise to ratchet up the level of combat, Garfield resigned his major generalcy, ended his active military career, and waited for the December start of Congress.

3

Congressional Career

Among the remarkable aspects of Garfield's eighteen-year congressional career was the political stability of the district he represented. Only once, in 1874, did his share of the total vote fall below 60 percent. This certainty of reelection, and the fact that Ohio was a key electoral state, helped Garfield and his aspirations for national Republican Party leadership. These political facts of life, when combined with his speaking abilities, instinctive winning ways, and friendships with Chase and other Washington bigwigs, marked Garfield for positions of influence and authority. Although he had no intention of initially making army matters the focus of his political career, Garfield's first assignment was a choice seat on the Committee on Military Affairs—a natural fit, given his service as a general in the Union army. And, since the Thirty-eighth Congress's principal concern was safeguarding and strengthening Union combat forces—to maintain relentless pressure on rebel troops—he became deeply involved in the business of running an army.

When the committee's chairman, Robert Schenck, a fellow Ohioan and widowed retired general, invited Garfield to room with him, the young congressman welcomed the opportunity. Their accommodations in a C Street boardinghouse became a miniature base camp; anybody who had financial dealings with the military seemed to show up on their doorstep. Contractors, generals, hangers-on, purveyors, all manner of men crowded the stairwells hoping to buttonhole the congressmen. Garfield's growing influence was obvious and, as he later recalled, the Military Affairs assignment provided "a prominence in the House in the beginning that I could not possibly have had in any other way."[1] The hardworking Garfield was learning the technical intricacies of how Congress governed: he managed the passage of a conscription bill (he was a strong supporter of the wartime draft and against paid substitutes, a practice that allowed a man to buy his way out of service); he sponsored a resolution of thanks to General Rosecrans for his service at Chickamauga (he realized that by having the nation express its gratitude he was also defending himself against the stigma of the military defeat); and he participated in the debate over equal pay for black soldiers (he favored equal pay retroactive to the date of enlistment for those who had been free men at the time of their enlistment, but retroactive pay only to the beginning of 1864 for all others).

Garfield's interest in military affairs did not overshadow his concern about the political issues surrounding Lincoln's conduct of the war. Despite the president's assurance that combat activities would intensify, Garfield, as one of the more radical of the radical Republicans, still regarded Lincoln's policies as too moderate. Garfield's increasing antipathy toward Lincoln was a marked change from his earlier opinion. Three years before, in February 1861, when the president-elect stopped off in Ohio as he made his way to Washington, Garfield had been favorably impressed. "He clearly shows his want of culture, and the marks of western life, but there is no touch of affectation in him," Garfield wrote to a friend. "[Lincoln's] remarkable good sense, simple and condensed style of expression, and evident marks of indomitable will, give me great hopes for the country."[2] However, two years later, when Lincoln issued the final Emancipation Proclamation in January 1863, Garfield was not so admiring. Garfield told the same friend that he found it a "strange phenomenon in the world's history, when a second-rate Illinois lawyer is the instrument to utter words which shall form an epoch

memorable in all future ages."[3] Garfield's less than flattering opinion of Lincoln continued when he refused to actively support Lincoln's reelection bid within the Republican Party. "He will probably
be the man," Garfield regretfully concluded, "though I think we
could do better."[4]

Garfield and the radical Republicans were further exasperated
by Lincoln's failure to back a policy of confiscation that would
place the property of Southern landowners in the possession of
Northerners. The radicals took the position that, by seceding, the
eleven Confederate states had forfeited all legal rights and were to
be regarded as little more than conquered territory with land and
chattel to be claimed by the victors. Rejecting Lincoln's position
that legal protections still applied in the rebellious states, the radicals voted through their own legislation, which ensured that plans
for reconstruction would be under Congress's direction rather than
the executive branch. Lincoln pocket-vetoed the measure. The radicals were furious and several of them dashed off an angry retort
(known as the Wade-Davis Manifesto) that appeared in the nation's
newspapers. They accused Lincoln of being a dictator with the sole
interest of personal gain. Matters worsened when Chase, Garfield's
political mentor, resigned from Lincoln's cabinet over a patronage
squabble. All of this occurred at a time when Lincoln's popularity
with the Northern voters was running high. Any attempt to criticize his course was resented by the Republican base as tantamount
to disloyalty to the government. Rumors ran rampant concerning
the political viability of the Republican-led administration. Indeed,
talk of a coup d'état was heard. In Garfield's Western Reserve district, his role in the episode was questioned, particularly his part in
the writing of the manifesto as well as other anti-Lincoln acts.

In August 1864, the stage was set for one of Garfield's greatest
public speaking successes. The Republican nominating convention
for Ohio's congressional delegation was in session and Garfield was
asked to address the people and explain his actions. Realizing that
his renomination hinged upon soothing an angered constituency,
Garfield gave what his wife would later term "the bravest speech in

his life."[5] He denied any role in writing or planting the opinion piece and even told the delegates that he thought the editorial was ill-timed. Nonetheless, he matter-of-factly informed the pro-administration listeners that Lincoln was not his first choice for the presidency. As reported by an eyewitness, Garfield then declared, "I hold it to be my privilege under the Constitution and as a man to criticize any acts of the President of the United States." More so, asserted Garfield, "I cannot go to Congress as your representative with my liberty restricted in this respect in any degree. If I go to Congress I must go as a free man."[6] The crowd was spellbound by Garfield's body language and words and, according to a newspaper reporter, those present rose to their feet and broke into resounding cheers. Within minutes, he was renominated by acclamation but not before the delegates passed a resolution condemning the radicals' anti-Lincoln deeds. Garfield's ultimate vindication came three months later when he was reelected by a three-to-one majority.

Garfield returned to Washington as both a Republican Party supporter and one of Lincoln's severest in-house critics. While condemning the president's conciliatory attitude toward the South, Garfield continued to vote with the party on most political and slavery issues. His hostility concerning Lincoln was somewhat mollified following the president's assassination in April 1865. "My heart is so broken with our great national loss that I can hardly think or write or speak," Garfield wrote to his wife. "I am sick at heart and feel it to be almost like sacrilege to talk of money or business now."[7] Despite his sadness over Lincoln's death, the war's end did not soften Garfield's views about reconstruction nor would he become a political ally of Andrew Johnson, Lincoln's successor.

Johnson's plan for reconstruction was closely patterned after Lincoln's and provided a broad amnesty to the seceding states. Many Northerners were dismayed to learn that under Johnson's arrangement, Southerners would be permitted to vote and that many of their political firebrands might soon return to the halls of Congress. In addition, the rebel states could impose new varieties of restrictions upon freed black Americans. The radical Republicans, believing that Johnson was effectively a Southern sympathizer, vigorously moved to defeat his program. Foremost among Garfield's concerns was the enfranchisement of freed blacks. He viewed voting rights and democracy as the surest method to secure the hard-won military victory. However, Northern sentiment in favor of black suffrage was far from universal. Speaking at a Fourth of July rally, Garfield conceded the political difficulties of granting elective franchise to what he termed "the great mass of ignorant and degraded blacks, so lately slaves." But, he told his audience, the ballot must be given to black Americans to protect them against social and physical injustices. "Let us not commit ourselves to the absurd and senseless dogma that the color of the skin shall be the basis of suffrage, the talisman of liberty."[8] Although public opinion remained lukewarm on the question of black suffrage, the radical Republicans passed the Civil Rights Act of 1866, which established citizenship for black Americans and forbade discrimination against them.

The breach between Johnson and the radical Republicans widened and calls for his impeachment began. With the radicals in control of Congress, they pushed through their own plan of reconstruction, placing the Southern states under military rule. In addition, the Republicans passed legislation calling for restrictions upon Johnson's power to appoint and remove members of his administration. When Johnson allegedly violated some of these restraints, the House voted a resolution of impeachment, which Garfield supported. As the trial began in the Senate, Garfield watched with interest. When the senators failed by one vote to impeach Johnson, Garfield was angered. He wrote to his friends about "the great betrayal" and how a "great wrong was consummated."[9] But Garfield reserved his strongest criticism for his erstwhile mentor Salmon Chase, who had become chief justice in 1864 and had presided over the Senate trial. Garfield felt that Chase had favored the defense. "It is the hardest thing I ever have to do," he told a friend, "to withdraw confidence and love from a man to whom I have once given them, but the conduct of Mr. Chase has been outrageous. . . .

I have no doubt he is trying to break the Republican party and make himself president."[10] Presidential politics were beginning to intrigue Garfield as he went about forming his own base of political power within the Congress.

With the conclusion of the fighting, many of the financial measures that had been enacted to fund the war needed to be reevaluated. A massive national debt required reconciliation; budgetary allowances for reconstruction of the defeated South had to be established; a wartime strategy of high tariffs and protectionism was in need of legislative overhaul; and questions concerning monetary policy, including the backing of money by gold and whether the Treasury should alleviate the nation's deficit by issuing paper currency or coin silver freely, called for congressional action. Garfield, ever ambitious, recognized that the management of the nation's finances involved important political decisions and that these often ended up as front-page news. As he sought a place on any House committee dealing with revenue questions, Garfield made much of the fact that Secretary of the Treasury Hugh McCulloch had stated publicly that he was the best-read representative on economic matters. Garfield was soon appointed to the powerful Committee of Ways and Means, followed by the chairmanship of the Committee on Banking and Currency.

Garfield's studious ways won him much praise. He was at ease reviewing financial spreadsheets, and he drew intellectual satisfaction from his understanding of the science of economics. To him, numbers may have been impassive, but they embodied the truth. Garfield also believed in fiscal pragmatism. "The government is an artificial giant and the power that moves it is money," he said in a speech before the House of Representatives. "Our national expenditures should be measured by the real necessities and the proper needs of the government. We should cut our garment so as to fit the person to be clothed."[11] Through his congressional years, Garfield remained firm in his conviction that the federal government should do nothing to create an unstable currency or to generate uncertainty concerning its own financial faith and credit.

The great monetary debate of the era centered on the status of paper money, so-called greenbacks, which the Treasury had issued to support the war effort. Also known as "fiat currency" because it was made legal tender by law or fiat (rather than by its intrinsic value, like precious metals), paper money was not backed by gold and was not redeemable in coin. Critics pointed out that greenbacks brought about inflation and drove gold-backed currency out of circulation. Indeed, detractors regarded the presence of fiat money as an absolute breach of financial faith on the part of the federal government. Supporters of greenbackism consisted mostly of the debtor classes, especially farmers, who wanted to issue greater amounts of paper currency and coin silver more freely in an attempt to produce inflation and reduce both personal and national liabilities. Ohio was an important battleground state in this political conflict between supporters of hard and soft money. Garfield, knowing that he was in a politically safe district, viewed the issues strictly in terms of economic logic, devoid of social implications. He concluded, much to the dismay of his Ohio soft-money supporters, that greenbacks should be reduced in quantity, with those left in circulation immediately backed by gold. Garfield, who opposed inflation, insisted that governmental deficits be settled in coin. A lucid ledger sheet was the expected goal.

Although these complex monetary issues would not be settled for many years, Garfield's stance made him a leader on the fiscally conservative side of the political debate. As he had hoped, national exposure soon followed. The widely read *Atlantic Monthly* published an article by him about the currency conflict, and he was asked to give speeches advocating his positions in cities throughout the United States. These lectures bolstered his image as a down-home westerner regarding social issues, but with a wealthy easterner's capitalistic outlook on economic questions. In fact, the born-on-a-farm Garfield even opposed cooperative farm ventures, labor unions, and their push for the eight-hour workday, as well as most federally funded relief projects. Garfield's advocacy of what he termed "sound" fiscal policies, based on his extensive readings and rooted in the experience of his committee assignments, would become an important factor in his obtaining the Republican presidential nomination in 1880.

Garfield's strongly held financial views also led to some of the greatest disappointments in his congressional career. Tariffs had emerged as a matter of importance to the various new industries that had sprung up during the war years. In response to these concerns, the Republican Party incorporated the need for a strong protective tariff as part of its election platform, and economic protectionists became a growing and controlling element in the party. Garfield was nominally a protectionist, albeit with little zeal, because he believed in free trade and a competitive marketplace. He promoted what might later be called the trickle-down theory of economic growth, whereby the government facilitates the expansion of business productivity on the assumption that all of society will eventually benefit. "I am for a protection which leads to ultimate free trade," he proclaimed, adding, "I am for that free trade which can be only achieved through protection."[12] In attempting to occupy some middle-ground position, Garfield found himself in a political conundrum and in a philosophical battle with his party's protectionists. When he supported a reduction of certain tariffs, his detractors became incensed. Garfield's perceived waffling contributed to his failure to gain an appointment as chairman of the Committee on Ways and Means, the one position in the House he truly desired. Though Garfield eventually headed the almost equally important Committee on Appropriations, as long as the Republicans held a majority in Congress, he never regained his seat on the Ways and Means Committee.

For many years Garfield blamed James G. Blaine, the Speaker of the House, for this slight. "There has been a heavy pressure brought to bear upon [Blaine] to keep me off the committee so that it may be made up more in the interest of the high tariff men," complained Garfield. "What Blaine will do I cannot tell. The impression is gaining ground that he is tricky."[13] Blaine had entered Congress in 1863, the same year as Garfield, and they had a great deal in common, including similar views on monetary legislation, reconstruction, and political control of patronage. But Blaine was less the thinker and more the doer than Garfield. Tall and erect, with a prominent nose, dark eyes, and a flashing smile, Blaine surpassed even Garfield's talents as a champion debater and convivial friend. Blaine had an infallible memory for names, faces, and places, and his organizational talents led to his becoming Speaker within five years of entering Congress. Garfield regarded Blaine as his major Republican rival and their careers remained closely intertwined.

The first half of the 1870s were Garfield's most influential years as a congressman. He was chairman of the crucial Committee on Appropriations and established himself as the fiscal watchdog of the House. "The expenditure of revenue and its distribution," according to Garfield, "form the best test of the health, the wisdom, and the virtue of a government."[14] He took an avid interest in issues relating to educational endeavors, calling for the establishment of a federal Department of Education and seeking to devote funds received from use of public lands toward such a project. He served on the boards of the Hampton Institute, Hiram College, and the Smithsonian Institution. Garfield helped finance federal scientific expeditions and was a major force behind the creation of the United States Geological Survey. The six-volume *Medical and Surgical History of the War of the Rebellion*, regarded as one of the most important works in the history of American medicine, was organized and published due to his insistence that money be made available for the project. By all accounts, Garfield had become a skillful and influential parliamentarian with a remarkable grasp of public issues.

It was also during the early 1870s, however, that three scandals scarred his career and brought Garfield unflattering national publicity. His involvement in these matters seemed strange at the time, since Garfield was decidedly puritanical in his views concerning public officials, industrialists, and illicit business dealings. This ethical strictness was especially evident when Garfield, as chairman of the Committee on Banking and Currency, investigated the well-publicized financial outrage known as "Black Friday" or the "Gold-Panic" episode, which had occurred in the fall of 1869. In this seedy incident, two Wall Street tycoons, having cultivated the friendship of President Ulysses S. Grant and his family, attempted to corner the nation's gold supply and reap enormous profits. Garfield scrutinized the situation and, in the report his committee issued in March 1870, did not hide the fact that the plotters relied on their closeness with the Grants. Outwardly oblivious to the political ramifications of his inquiries, Garfield privately remarked, "The abysses of wickedness which are opening before us in the investigation are among the most remarkable things I have met."[15] In the final analysis, Garfield failed to establish any direct link between the conspirators and Grant himself. But Garfield was well aware of the taint that scandal could have on a political career and how such matters needed to be handled. "I may say," Garfield wrote to a friend, "that the President expresses himself under a good many obligations to me for the management of the Gold Panic investigation."[16]

But two years later, in the summer of 1872, Garfield faced accusations concerning his own dishonesty when he was revealed as a participant in the Crédit Mobilier affair. This matter, one of the most notorious scandals in American history, involved the peddling of stock in a dummy corporation to members of Congress in an attempt to forestall legislative inquiry into the company's finances. The investigation concerned the government's subsidizing of tens of millions of dollars to build the Union Pacific Railroad from Nebraska to Utah. Several influential stockholders of the Union Pacific organized another company, the Crédit Mobilier of America, to surreptitiously siphon off any profits from the construction. It was a fraudulent scheme from the beginning that depleted all of the generous congressional grants and left the railroad with insurmountable debts.

The scandal became political when some of the Crédit Mobilier stock was used as hush money in the halls of Congress. Conspicuous on the list of supposedly bribed congressmen was Garfield. A

House investigating committee asked Garfield and fifteen other legislators to explain their dealings with Crédit Mobilier. Some denied their involvement, others admitted to being mixed up in the deal, and Garfield gave an ambiguous answer. When the investigators delivered their report, they concluded that Garfield was guilty of accepting ten shares of stock, but that his interest in the company was minimal and that it had not affected his congressional duties. Indeed, Garfield's real offense was that he knowingly denied to the House investigating committee that he had agreed to accept the stock and that he had also received a dividend of $329. To Garfield's way of thinking, it was all an innocent mistake since, at the time of the gift, he had no idea what Crédit Mobilier was, nor did the shares ever influence his political decisions. A House vote to censure Garfield failed. Editorials lambasted him for his less-than-honest answers. "Well, the wickedness of all of it," the *New York Tribune* wrote, "is that these men betrayed the trust of the people, deceived their constituents, and by their evasions and falsehoods confessed the transaction to be disgraceful."[17]

Garfield was flummoxed, especially since he had had no meaningful connection with the company. He always considered his actions to be above suspicion and his testimony an honest accounting. "I am too proud to confess to any but my most intimate friends how deeply this whole matter has grieved me," he wrote in his diary. "While I did nothing in regard to it that can be construed into any act even of impropriety much less than corruption, I have still said from the start that the shadow of the cursed thing would cling to my name for many years."[18] Garfield was prescient in his prediction; the Crédit Mobilier morass would be used against him in his run for the presidency. For now, however, his political troubles were just beginning.

Garfield assumed that his immediate task was to explain Crédit Mobilier to his Ohio constituents. He was mistaken. The voters were more upset over what was called the "Salary Grab of 1873." The congressional membership had just voted itself a 50 percent salary increase, from $5,000 to $7,500 per year, including retroactive pay to the beginning of the session two years earlier. At the time of the approval, nearly half of the legislators were lame ducks, or nonreturning, which meant they would be leaving the House with a $5,000 going-away present. Press and public reaction was furious, since they associated the "salary grab" with the climate of corruption that had surrounded the Crédit Mobilier case.

The charges would take their political toll and Garfield, as chairman of the Committee on Appropriations, was singled out as the chief culprit. Many of Ohio's farm families, who were having difficulty meeting their mortgage obligations, regarded the salary increase and the retroactive pay as the equivalent to stealing. "To my surprise I find that just now there is more agitation in regard to my vote on the increase of salaries of members of Congress than there is in regard to Crédit Mobilier," Garfield told his wife. "I cannot tell whether it is the hour of breaking up or not. I shall try to meet manfully whatever comes to my lot; but it is hard to bear the small talk of little carpers who know nothing of the case."[19] But the fault finders were not going to stop, and friends urged him to mount a vigorous defense.

Garfield wrote a letter to the Republican voters of his district, setting forth his side of the story. He criticized the handling of the salary increase, but was quick to point out that every past congressional raise included a retroactive increase applied to the whole term of the Congress that authorized it. "It was not a crime," he said, "and we have no right to say that those who advocated it were thieves and robbers."[20] Garfield never accepted the back pay and, although he initially opposed the salary increase, as chairman he ultimately guided it through the House. The salary increase was a minor portion of that year's total appropriation bill, and Garfield disingenuously claimed an obligation to defend the whole proposal to prevent Congress from having to schedule a special session simply to rework the budget. Garfield's judgment was open to question, and many observers considered him politically dead. But this was not true. He was fortunate that the Crédit Mobilier scandal had come too late to derail his reelection in 1872 and that the "salary grab" controversy erupted eighteen months before the 1874 race. "It is too late to retire; the battle is set and must go on," Garfield reflected in his diary. "The year 1873 has, like myself, suffered some hard knocks and abuses and passes into oblivion scarred and bruised and not greatly regretted."[21]

By the spring of 1874, it appeared that Garfield had outlasted his enemies. Blaine, the Speaker of the House, retained him as chairman of the Committee on Appropriations and gave him an additional assignment to the influential Rules Committee. Garfield's mood was upbeat when he wrote one Ohioan, "I know that I have done [the people of the district] more efficient service this winter than at any other time since I have been in public life."[22] But he had one more scandal to weather and this one was entirely of his own making. The year before, Garfield had been asked to represent the DeGolyer-McClelland Company in its bid for a contract with the District of Columbia's Board of Public Works to construct a patented system of wooden sidewalks. Garfield had an obvious conflict of interest. As chairman of the Committee on Appropriations, he was partially responsible for the monetary affairs of the District of Columbia and should have known better than to take on this particular client. After a persistent lobbying campaign, DeGolyer-McClelland was awarded the contract and Garfield received a $5,000 fee.

At first, since Garfield was a practicing attorney, little appeared sordid in the arrangement. Washington was an expensive city in which to live, and it was not unusual for members of Congress who were not independently wealthy (as was Garfield's case) to pursue a second occupation. The difficulty came from the size of the fee in relation to what was considered the small amount of expended effort. More important, reporters soon discovered that, supposedly unbeknownst to Garfield, he had been asked to represent DeGolyer-McClelland more for his powerful position in Congress than for his legal talents. Garfield was indignant at charges that he had acted corruptly. "I propose to stand on my rights as an American citizen," he told a friend. "There is nothing either of law or

morals to prohibit a member of Congress from practicing his profession."[23]

Garfield was naive, and although his actions did not speak to
true corruption or dishonesty, they demonstrated poor judgment.
His involvement in the DeGolyer scheme was ripe for exploitation
by his political enemies. Garfield returned to Ohio prepared to
fight for his reelection. He became a whirlwind of activity, giving
speech after speech and explaining his position. He told the audi-
ences that the money for DeGolyer-McClelland did not directly
depend on national appropriations but was subject to the control of
a local legislature. Moreover, he was a licensed attorney who investigated the patent issues in the case and had spent, at least in his
opinion, a considerable amount of time studying the situation. "I
have had a hard and exhausting campaign," he wrote to a friend in
the weeks preceding the election, "but I shall beat the rascals who
have been opposing me."[24]

Garfield's 1874 campaign worked brilliantly as he stumped
through the district. His opponents challenged him to a series of
debates, but he refused. "I do not propose to allow these fellows to
get up at meetings and take up half the time throwing mud at
me."[25] On Election Day, Garfield received 57 percent of the vote. It
was a remarkable victory, particularly in light of the violent anti-
Republican reaction throughout the North that resulted in a Democratic landslide. "In view of the general deluge that has swept over
the party," he wrote a friend, "and in view of the bitter and malig-
nant assaults made upon me I feel that I came out better than could
have been expected. I am resting and reading Goethe's biography
and letting the calm of his great life fall into my own."[26]

As a result of the election of 1874, the House passed into Democratic hands for the first time since the Civil War. Blaine was out as
Speaker and was shortly elected to the Senate. Garfield, who was
no longer chairman of the Committee on Appropriations, was
appointed by the Democrats as a minority member of the Committee on Ways and Means. He became its ranking minority member
and the acknowledged spokesman for the Republican Party in the

House of Representatives. By merely surviving the election debacle and proving that he was among his party's steadiest vote-getters, the forty-three-year-old Garfield emerged as one of the more powerful figures in Washington. Now regarded as an influential Republican Party insider, Garfield soon found himself deeply involved in the presidential election of 1876.

During the previous few years, a series of events had thrown the country into political disarray. Grant's Republican administration had experienced an unprecedented number of scandals and he took himself out of the running for a third term. The nation found itself in a profound business depression, and the unsettled monetary and tariff issues had splintered the Republican Party's East-West coalition. Further clouding the political climate, the traditional Democratic hold on the South was threatened by a solid Republican black vote. A divided electorate was presented with confusing choices, including the emergence of fairly significant third parties. Against this backdrop, the Democrats hoped to make political gain out of the economic turndown and the Republican scandals. Their presidential nominee was Governor Samuel Tilden of New York, who was widely credited with having smashed Manhattan's corrupt Tweed ring. The Republicans, in a turbulent nominating process, selected Governor Rutherford B. Hayes of Ohio. Garfield, although not a strong Hayes supporter, remained a committed party loyalist. "I do not close my eyes to the fact that we have a hard and close contest before us," he wrote to Hayes. "I will give all the time I have to the coming campaign and hope you will communicate to me at any time any wish or suggestion."[27]

Garfield's work during the 1876 presidential election proved grueling. He was on the stump through most of Maine, New Jersey, upstate New York, and his own district in Ohio. Luckily for Garfield, his own reelection was assured. For Hayes and Tilden, the vote turned into electoral chaos. On the morning after the election, Tilden's popular majority was more than 260,000 votes. He had carried several key northern states, including New York, New Jersey, and Connecticut, and had 184 electoral votes to Hayes's 165.

However, another twenty electoral votes were in dispute due to supposed voting irregularities in Florida, Louisiana, and South Carolina. Official returns from these states favored Tilden, but the Republican-dominated state electoral commissions subsequently disallowed a sufficient number of cast votes to award their electoral votes to Hayes. This led to each state having to deliver to Congress two sets of electoral votes, one certified by the state's governor (favoring Hayes) and the other certified by the state's legislature (favoring Tilden). A constitutional crisis arose, and partisanship was at a peak.

In the middle of the political machinations was a resolute Garfield. He was "tired of the namby-pamby way in which many of our Republicans treat public questions," he wrote a friend.[28] Because a congressional procedure for resolving disputed sets of electors was not in place, Congress established a special fifteen-member electoral commission to decide the issue in each of the three states. Five members came from each house of Congress, with the majority party in each body (Democrats in the House and Republicans in the Senate) receiving three of the five members, and they were joined by five members of the United States Supreme Court (three Republican-appointed justices and two Democratic appointees). Garfield was the first choice of House Republicans to serve on their portion of the commission, even though the Democrats objected to him as extreme and biased. "If they expect to find a man who has no opinions on the subject," Garfield complained to an acquaintance, "they will certainly have to go outside of either house of Congress."[29] Despite the Democrats' concerns, he assumed the commission assignment without delay.

Following several weeks of partisan intrigue, the members of the special commission voted along party lines. In three separate eight-to-seven votes, the commissioners upheld Hayes's electors in the disputed southern states. Thus, Hayes was elected president. So intense was the Democratic outrage that an escort rode with Garfield in his carriage to the safety of his home to prevent his assassination. "You can scarcely imagine the intensity of feeling among the Democrats over the findings of the Commission," Garfield told a friend. "I may say to you (but not to be made public) that my friends have been anxious for my personal safety for many days."[30]

The Democrats, responding to the politicization of the Electoral Commission, threatened to filibuster acceptance of the report. Secret negotiations between Republican and Democratic politicians were held and a compromise was reached: southern Democrats would acknowledge Hayes as president if the Republicans consented to the removal of federal troops from all former Confederate states. In addition, at least one southern Democrat would be appointed to Hayes's cabinet and legislation to help industrialize the South would be passed. The Hayes-Tilden Compromise of 1877 brought an end to the process of Reconstruction in the former rebel states. It also secured the long-term dominance of the Democratic Party in the South as its members replaced Republican "carpetbagger" governments.

In both the North and the South, few individuals were more closely involved with resolving the presidential election imbroglio than Garfield. He made a highly publicized trip south to end the election confusion, and this, along with his resolve in the face of Democratic demands, made Garfield one of the era's most talked-about politicians. There was even a rumor that the Democrats, as a secret condition of the compromise, would allow Garfield to become Speaker of the House. Nothing was further from the truth, and Garfield, who at Hayes's request publicly turned down an opportunity to run for the Senate from Ohio, remained in the House. "On the whole I am not certain what the general verdict will be," Garfield confided in his diary. "I have some doubts whether the public will appreciate my motive."[31]

Hayes wanted Garfield to remain in the House for one simple reason: the House was controlled by the Democrats, and Hayes needed Garfield's political expertise and stature to counter the opposition's legislative initiatives. Garfield acquiesced to Hayes's wish primarily out of party loyalty but also with the ulterior motive of his own future success in mind. As the president's key legislator, Garfield's personal prestige would increase beyond that of anything he previously had. However, a problem soon arose: the two men began to have disputes over political policies. Hayes's dour and formal personality did not help matters, especially when contrasted with Garfield's warmth and gregariousness.

Garfield had strong reservations, for example, regarding the president's strategy on civil service reform. He disliked the Hayes policy that forbade federal civil servants from taking an active part in politics. In addition, he felt that the president was moving too quickly in his own patronage appointments, particularly Carl Schurz as secretary of the Treasury, and creating rifts between rival factions within the Republican Party. "It is surprising with what strength the current of public sentiment is turning against [Hayes]," noted Garfield. "I think his vague notions of Civil Service Reform, and his wretched practice upon it, has wrought the chief mischief with his administration."[32] Hayes refused to listen and Republican squabbling intensified. In March 1878, Garfield recorded in his diary, "I incline to believe that [Hayes's] election has been an almost fatal blow to his party."[33]

As the ranking House Republican, Garfield was obsessive about maintaining party unity. Voters in the North, however, rebuffed Hayes's policies, contributing to a Democratic sweep of Congress in the 1878 midterm election. A discouraged Garfield was ready for a career change as a chastened Hayes announced that he would not be a candidate for reelection in 1880. At the same time, Ohio's Republican leaders nominated Garfield as their choice for an open Senate seat. This time, Garfield welcomed the opportunity because he did not want observers to say that he was afraid to relinquish his secure House seat in lieu of a more difficult Senate race. Furthermore, he was working extremely long hours as the minority leader and looked forward to what he believed would be the relative quiet of the Senate. Finally, Garfield thought it unfair to other men in his district who aspired to the House to hold on to his position when the prospects of securing the senatorship were excellent. Moreover,

President Hayes no longer stood in his way. In January 1880, Garfield was easily elected by the Ohio legislature to the United States Senate. Almost 1,500 people greeted him in Columbus when he attended a reception in his honor in the Ohio Senate Chamber. Praised by pro-Republican papers in the state and feted by his constituents, Garfield's name was even mentioned as a dark horse candidate to replace the retiring Hayes.

4

The Private Garfield

In 1876, James and Lucretia Garfield bought a farm in Mentor, Ohio. Later dubbed "Lawnfield" by reporters because of the wide expanse of lawn on which they camped out during the 1880 presidential campaign, this ramshackle property provided the Garfields' marriage, according to one biographer, "a zest that knew no flagging."[1] Although together for almost twenty years, the Garfields' relationship had experienced its ups and downs. In the 1860s, there had been rumors of Garfield's persistent philandering. Lucretia warned her husband "to let the fire of such lawless passion burn itself out, unfed and unnoticed."[2] Even as late as 1880, the Garfields were forced to publicly deny gossip about an impending divorce. Throughout his life, Garfield maintained intensely close relationships with a number of women. Certainly, the stories concerning Garfield's early emotional infidelities were true. James seemed to verify the hearsay when he wrote Lucretia, "Let me once again thank you that by your grand faith and truth and endurance our love was saved and purified through the fiery ordeal of the years."[3] Whether any of these associations included a sexual element remains historical conjecture.

Despite their early difficulties, the middle and later years of the Garfields' marriage were marked by a strong sense of togetherness and familial bonding. Indeed, Garfield wrote to a friend, "You should polarize your life by love and marriage and home."[4] The physical inconveniences and financial difficulties of living apart prompted the Garfields, in 1869, to build a squarish brick house on the northeast corner of Thirteenth and I Streets in Washington. "I am sure if our home should be really finished and you permitted to take me into it," wrote Lucretia, "I shall feel more than ever before that I am your wedded wife taken to your hearth and heart."[5] This three-story residence, enlarged in 1878, served as their domestic base and social center when Congress was in session.

The Garfields grew into a large, close-knit family with seven children, five of whom survived into adulthood. Garfield's mother, a domineering, doting, and opinionated woman, lived with them, having joined the Washington household after accusing her son of not properly caring for her. Eliza Garfield's presence and intolerant disposition caused considerable family friction. Garfield's daughter Mollie would later write of her grandmother, "Such a woman as she is, I just can't stand."[6] Despite these minor family tensions, every year brought Garfield increasing marital happiness as he and Lucretia reveled in the growth and intelligence of their children.

Summers were spent on the farm in Mentor, which provided a refuge from the everyday hustle and bustle of Washington politics. Over the years, the main dwelling at Lawnfield was refurbished and expanded and the Garfield family spent lengthy amounts of time on the property. "You can hardly imagine," Garfield wrote from Mentor, "how completely I have turned my mind out of its usual channels during the last four weeks. You know I have never been able to do anything moderately; and today I find myself lame in every muscle with too much lifting and digging."[7] The farmhouse was eventually equipped with its own telegraph line, and the front porch would serve as the stage for much of Garfield's campaign for the presidency.

Despite Lawnfield's appeal, with its sights and sounds of a simple farm life and Lucretia's plain-cooked meals, Garfield was very much a public man who had great difficulty separating his political and private obligations. He had a restless personality and was constantly searching for the next career challenge. His various admirers portrayed him as a hardworking intellect, and the daily records of the Library of Congress show that he signed out more books and spent a greater amount of time there than any other congressman. Visitors to the house in Washington always remarked on the size of Garfield's study, which overflowed with well-thumbed volumes and was scattered with research material on the workings of the federal government. "They confront you in the hall when you enter, in the parlor and the sitting-room, in the dining-room and even in the bath-room, where documents and speeches are corded up like firewood," remarked one guest.[8] The range of his reading was enormous, and Garfield always made certain that he had books with him when he traveled. "He was animated by an intense and sleepless spirit of acquisition," said one of his admirers. "His ambition was for the acquisition of knowledge. From early youth to the day of his last illness it was a consuming passion."[9] Garfield became a classics scholar, and many observers agreed he was the most well-educated congressman of that era. In one apocryphal but widely spread tale, intended to demonstrate Garfield's intellectual prowess, he was said to amaze friends by simultaneously writing Greek with one hand and Latin with the other.

The amount of time that Garfield spent preparing speeches, writing letters, lobbying for his constituents, or readying himself for a debate in the House of Representatives was staggering. And, as could be anticipated, he was inevitably the best prepared. James Blaine described him as a "steady and indefatigable worker." "Those who imagine that talent or genius can supply the place or achieve the results of labor," cautioned Blaine, "will find no encouragement in Garfield's life."[10] Even Garfield's work as a part-time lawyer was acknowledged as exemplary—DeGolyer-McClelland notwithstanding—and brought him legal fame and a place in the constitutional law books.

Among his cases, *Ex Parte Milligan* remains one of the most celebrated in American judicial history. Arguing before the Supreme Court of the United States in 1866, Garfield and several other attorneys represented a group of petitioners—penniless, civilian Confederate sympathizers from Indiana—who were tried, convicted, and sentenced to death by a military court for having engaged in treasonous activities. The major issue before the Supreme Court was not the veracity of the original charges, but the right of military tribunals to try and condemn civilians in areas remote from the war zone, where ordinary civil courts were in session. The court ruled for the petitioners on the grounds that, under the circumstances prevailing in Indiana at the time of their offense, they should have been tried in a civilian court. Garfield's fellow radical Republicans were enraged by both the ruling and the fact that he was one of the defense lawyers for a group of traitors. What particularly irked the radicals were fears that the case would establish a legal precedent that could hamper the military's role in reconstruction in the South. Such a political scenario never occurred. Moreover, Garfield went out of his way to assure his radical friends that he would continue to support their legislative strategies concerning the South. He made it well known that he received no money for this particular case (he even paid for the printing of his legal brief and arguments) and was simply acting as an attorney defending a client. However, each year Garfield's part-time practice of law provided several thousand dollars of necessary supplementary income. "I have always found a keen intellectual pleasure in the law," Garfield confessed in his diary. "It reaches out into what is impersonal, it is unpartisan, and may be so studied as to enlarge the spirit. I am conscious of not being fitted for the partisan work of politics, although I believe in partisanship, within reasonable limits."[11]

Garfield's self-assessment was accurate. As he grew older and assumed more political responsibilities, he tried to avoid partisan confrontations. Both his adversaries and supporters called him morally weak and hesitant in his decision making. "His willpower was not equal to his personal magnetism," recollected one Ohio Republican. "He easily changed his mind and honestly veered from one impulse to another."[12] This charge of indecisiveness was not altogether reasonable. If Garfield did shift his views on certain issues, he was just as likely to be tenacious on others. Garfield was long adamant that his religious views—he was affiliated with the Disciples of Christ—not color his political beliefs. "I would rather be defeated than make Capital out of my Religion," he stated during his presidential campaign.[13] Certainly, his opinions on money matters and military reconstruction of the South, among the major questions of the 1860s and 1870s, never varied. In fairness, what was considered political vacillation was Garfield's determination to understand the various sides of an issue by reason rather than emotion. There was one character trait, however, that all agreed was a mainstay of his personality: a sensitivity to criticism. For an influential public figure who was often in the spotlight, Garfield was remarkably thin-skinned. He constantly sought approval of his actions from supporters, reporters, and family, and, if not satisfied to the truthfulness of their praise, often became despondent. "I don't suppose I shall ever get the credit I deserve for [my intellectual work]," he lamented to a friend. "On the whole I am inclined to the opinion that the popular estimate of intellectual work is in the inverse ratio of its real value."[14]

By the spring of 1880, despite talk concerning his character flaws, Garfield was recognized as one of the ablest and most effective legislators of his generation. He was viewed as a leader of national stature, who provided a breadth of view not common to the average Gilded Age politician. Garfield had worked hard through the years and was a successful party strategist whom influential insiders regarded highly. Despite protestations to the contrary, he enjoyed knowing that his name was occasionally mentioned as warranting a spot on the national ticket in the upcoming presidential election.

5

The Presidential
Election of 1880

Garfield was an ambitious politician, but the possibility of securing the top position on the national ticket seemed remote. By February 1880, three candidates were touted as front-runners for the Republican nomination: former president Ulysses S. Grant; James G. Blaine, Garfield's old party rival; and John Sherman, secretary of the Treasury. Early on, Garfield removed himself from the immediacy of the race by publicly declaring his support for Sherman and agreeing to become his spokesman at the nominating convention. It was a deft political move that seemed to underscore Garfield's private affirmations that he was not interested in the presidency and did not wish to create a dark horse candidacy. "I long ago made a resolution that I would never permit myself to let the Presidential fever get any lodgement in my brain," he wrote to a friend. "I think it is the one office in this nation that for his own peace no man ought to set his heart upon."[1]

Sherman, the younger brother of the renowned Civil War general William Tecumseh Sherman, had served as U.S. senator from Ohio before becoming a member of Hayes's cabinet. He and Garfield had been friends for over twenty years and Garfield had won his new seat in the Senate primarily through Sherman's auspices. In helping to place Garfield in the Senate, Sherman hoped to sidetrack any possibility of Garfield emerging as the convention's

alternative nominee, especially as a favorite son from Ohio, following a three-way deadlock. Privately, Garfield doubted Sherman's
ability to win the nomination but thought that Sherman's presence
in the balloting would block Grant's nomination. As an added
inducement for Garfield's support, Sherman promised that if he
could not be nominated, he was willing to transfer his entire convention strength to Garfield if he should emerge as a compromise
candidate. Indeed, by supporting Sherman and becoming his spokesman, Garfield realized that he was establishing himself among the
most visible of the party's potential compromise candidates.

Despite Garfield's public and private denials of interest, a run
for the White House in 1880 remained for him a reasonable aspira-
tion. Five years earlier, he and Lucretia had discussed the possibility
of such a campaign, but the timing seemed wrong. During the
Hayes administration, Garfield's name was mentioned by admiring
friends and political sycophants as worthy of presidential consideration. Hayes even went so far as to talk about Garfield's presidential
prospects during a train trip the two men took in 1878. But Garfield, the party loyalist and committed Sherman supporter, refused
to acknowledge any of the gossip.

Regardless of his disclaimers, admirers continued to clamor for a
Garfield candidacy. In early February, the governor of Wisconsin
told Garfield that some of his state's delegates wished to organize a
campaign for Garfield's nomination. Two weeks later, a group of
influential Pennsylvanians met with Garfield to outline their convention predictions and plans. They anticipated a back-and-forth
balloting scenario that would result in a deadlock among Blaine,
Grant, and Sherman. Stuck with a stalemate, the delegates would
look to Garfield, the most well known of the dark horse candidates.
According to a participant at this meeting, Garfield agreed with
their scenario and acquiesced to their strategies, with the caveat
that his knowledge of them remain a secret. Garfield's diary, however, reveals a different rendition: "I told them I would not be a candidate, and did not wish my name discussed in that connection," he
wrote. "If anything happened to me in that connection it would

only be in case the Convention at Chicago could not nominate either of the candidates and I should do nothing to procure such a result."[2]

Garfield might not have wanted the public or party insiders to think of him as a dark horse candidate, but he paid close attention to the preconvention machinations. Indeed, less than a month before the delegates arrived in Chicago, having been assailed in newspaper editorials for a recent congressional vote on import taxes, Garfield acknowledged his status. "The charge is utterly groundless," he wrote in his diary. "I think it is an effort of some interested parties to hurt me just now, in view of some loose talk in the papers mentioning me as a dark horse."[3] Not only did the personal attacks increase but, as the clamor for Garfield's candidacy grew, he did little to halt the groundswell of support. "The signs have multiplied that the Convention is strongly turning its attention to me," Garfield wrote his wife. "Large numbers of men are confident that will be the result. I should think there was something in it."[4]

In retrospect, two contrasting viewpoints about Garfield's nomination for the presidency have emerged. According to the first, the selection came to Garfield as a complete shock and represented little more than the wearied end result of fruitless ballots that necessitated the emergence of a compromise candidate. In the opinion of other observers, Garfield was, from the outset, a secret contender. He obtained the nomination by first misleading Sherman and then, through his own political shrewdness, led the delegates to regard him as a dark horse. With unusual perspicacity, Garfield's silent candidacy was planned with careful attention to the political happenings of the day. The truth probably lies somewhere between these two scenarios, but, regardless of which is believed, the Republican convention of 1880 was marked by antagonism, controversy, and subterfuge.

When Garfield arrived in Chicago, he was convinced that the greatest danger to the party's chances of winning in November was the nomination of Grant. Grant's presidency had been uninspiring and his eight years in the White House had been mired in scandal and economic downturns. To distance himself from these difficulties, Grant had embarked on a two-and-a-half-year trip around the world. Everywhere he traveled, the ex-president was received as a great war hero. American newspaper accounts, detailing the heartfelt nature of these receptions, helped renew the popularity that Grant previously enjoyed. On his return, conniving Republican bosses, led by Senator Roscoe Conkling of New York, saw in Grant's rising esteem—and his political naïveté—an opportunity to win a third term for the general, and to exploit, for their own underhanded purposes, the incoming administration.

Conkling, an unpleasant individual, used his senatorial powers to ride roughshod over party underlings. He never forgot a slight and was uninterested in the process of conciliation. Arrogant, condescending, vain—he was tall and handsome with silver hair and a perfectly coiffed beard—and an unrepentant womanizer, Conkling prided himself on controlling federal patronage within the state of New York. Similarly, he attempted to dominate the New York delegates to the 1880 convention by pushing for the unit rule, whereby each state's votes would be recorded as a block for the candidate receiving the majority of the votes within the delegation. In contrast to the previously used district rule, in which the choice of each elector was individually counted, the imposition of the unit rule was seen as a ploy by party bosses to defeat Republican factionism and preserve their influence.

Republican infighting had produced two major ideological groups. The Stalwart faction, led by Conkling, was originally named because its members were unyielding in their opposition to Hayes's policy regarding Southern Reconstruction. These men also opposed civil service reform and supported continuance of the spoils system. Under this system of patronage, appointed offices were the booty of the party in power, to be distributed with opportunities for profit among the party faithful, without regard to merit. The

Stalwarts were similarly unwavering in their advocacy of Grant's bid for a third term. Since it was common knowledge that the former president did not enjoy the backing of a majority of the convention's delegates, adoption of the boss-backed, Stalwart-supported unit rule would go far toward ensuring a Grant nomination. The other main bloc, the Half-Breeds, were more moderate in their views and accepted some degree of civil service reform, albeit in a piecemeal fashion. The term "Half-Breed" originated as an insult against a group of Republicans, organized around Blaine, who had wavered in their loyalty to Grant during his term as president. It later turned into a compliment as Grant's administration faltered.

Garfield was outraged at the unfairness of unit rule and, as a leader of the anti-Grant forces—Garfield was sympathetic to the Half-Breeds but did not regard himself as a bona fide member— came into direct confrontation with Conkling. The Garfield-Conkling conflict was further aggravated by growing talk of derailing Grant's chances with a Garfield nomination. "You can hardly imagine the embarrassment I have been in from the moment of my arrival here by the number of delegates from all quarters who are openly expressing the wish that I was the Ohio candidate," Garfield wrote to his wife. "Many are firmly of the belief that all the candidates will be dropped and that I will be taken up."[5] By the convention's opening day, it took little more than the slightest mention of Garfield's name to elicit applause and raucous cheering throughout the auditorium.

The fight against Grant and the unit rule was taken to the convention's Rules Committee, which happened to be chaired by Garfield. In a stormy three-hour session, Garfield and the anti-Grant forces succeeded in passing a recommendation against the unit rule. As Garfield ominously told Lucretia, the fight "will be likely to embitter [Conkling] and his followers against me."[6] Having been defeated in this vital preconvention battle, and realizing that Grant's nomination was growing more doubtful, a still unyielding Conkling demanded that a variation of the unit rule issue be brought before the entire convention. The next day, he proposed a resolution requiring all delegates to be honor bound to support the convention's nominee. Any delegate who disagreed with this principle would forfeit his seat. Having lost the struggle over the unit rule, Conkling broached the resolution as a final and inconsequential effort to coerce delegates into supporting a third-term nomination for Grant. The delegates, recognizing that Conkling's proposal accomplished little more than unanimity following the balloting, passed it on a voice vote. But, when a few voices were heard to dissent, an out-of-control Conkling demanded that these individuals be punished.

Conkling's vindictiveness brought forth boos and hisses. An indignant Garfield, sensing the spreading anti-Conkling and anti-Grant mood, rose to his feet and slowly walked to the podium. A hushed quiet fell over the crowd. "I fear this Convention is about to commit a great error. . . . We come here as Republicans and as one of our rights we can vote on every resolution 'Aye' or 'No,'" he told the delegates. "I say [the dissenters] acted in their right and not by my vote shall they be deprived of their seats or their freedom."[7] Cries of "No! No!" to the Conkling proposal reverberated in the hall as the din of cheers for Garfield grew louder.[8] Garfield had made one of the great oratorical triumphs of his career in front of every important Republican in the land. "General Garfield won a fine reception today," wrote a newspaper reporter. "There is hope in all quarters that he will come actively to the front before the convention ends and there is no doubt but that hope will be gratified."[9] Conkling's suggestion was quickly tabled. More important, the New Yorker recognized the immediate implications of the moment. As Garfield left the dais, Conkling gave him a handwritten note: "New York requests that Ohio's real candidate and dark horse come forward."[10]

On the fourth evening of the convention, standing on a reporter's table in the blue cigar-smoke-filled Exposition Hall, surrounded by almost 800 delegates and over 15,000 onlookers, Conkling placed Grant's name in nomination. "Never defeated in peace or in war, his name is the most illustrious borne by living man," shouted the senator from New York. "With him as our leader we shall have no defensive campaign. No! We shall have nothing to explain away. We shall have no apologies to make."[11] It was speechmaking at its best but, in the usual sarcastic Conkling style, contained enough negatives about other candidates that it served only to further stiffen the anti-Grant forces.

Garfield's turn came next. He realized that to compare Sherman's accomplishments to Grant or even Blaine was out of the question. Instead, he extolled Sherman as a party loyalist who would win the election by uniting all Republicans. "We want the vote of every Republican—of every Grant Republican, and every Anti-Grant Republican, in America—of every Blaine man and every anti-Blaine man," urged Garfield. "The vote of every follower of every candidate is needed to make our success certain." In the middle of his exhortation, he asked, "And now, gentlemen of the Convention, what do we want?" A lone voice from the gallery called out, "We want Garfield." Prolonged applause erupted and a flustered Garfield asked the crowd for silence. "Bear with me a moment. Hear me for my cause and for a moment be silent that you may hear."[12] If there was doubt in anyone's mind as to Garfield's dark horse status, it was probably erased by this single incident. Garfield went on to nominate Sherman, but the drama of his oration made a profound impression on the conventioneers. As a later biographer wrote, "While he spoke, hundreds of the delegates who sat there felt that they were listening to the possible nominee of the convention, rather than the advocate of a candidate."[13]

Balloting for the presidential candidates began on the morning of June 5, a bright, cool, and delightful Monday. No observers expected a first ballot victory and, when the clerk completed calling the role of states, the numbers matched the predictions: Grant, 304; Blaine, 284; Sherman, 93—with 379 required for the nomination. Convention rules called for an immediate second ballot, but the vote totals remained essentially unchanged; the partisans of the candidates would not yield in favor of party unity. Beginning with the second ballot, however, Garfield's name was kept constantly in the delegates' minds by one or two votes from his Pennsylvania admirers. Thirteen hours and twenty-eight ballots later, with the vote totals fixed, the weary delegates adjourned, no closer to a decision than they had been weeks and even months before.

Political intrigue filled the night as deal makers worked to break the deadlock. Sherman came under intense pressure to withdraw in favor of Blaine or Garfield but he refused. Conkling and the Grant forces remained resolute. On Tuesday morning, five more ballots were completed, but with little change. This was the dreaded deadlock that Garfield's supporters had anticipated and hoped to exploit. On the next ballot, the thirty-fourth, members of the Wisconsin delegation, occupying a prominent position at the alphabetical end of the voting list, unexpectedly gave sixteen votes to Garfield. Political observers and historians have never determined what caused the Wisconsin switch, but on hearing the changed votes, Garfield sprang to his feet and demanded to speak. "I rise to a point of order. I challenge the correctness of the announcement," Garfield said. "The announcement contains votes for me. No man has a right without the consent of the person voted for, to announce that person's name and vote for him in this convention. Such consent I have not given."[14] At this point, the chairman of the convention, and a Garfield friend, ordered him to resume his seat, pronouncing him out of order. Some observers say Garfield looked stunned, while others accused him of acting out a long-rehearsed role. Immediately, the chairman declared that no person had received a majority of the votes cast and another ballot should be taken. On the next ballot, the Indiana delegates changed to Garfield, who ended up with fifty votes. At this point Sherman acquiesced, and, as he promised he would do if he could not be nominated, threw his support to Garfield. With the thirty-sixth ballot, a flood of Blaine and Sherman supporters switched to Garfield and the dark horse candidate had a majority and the nomination.

Pandemonium broke out and a fusillade of cannons was fired in

celebration. The crowd was on its feet chanting, "Garfield, Garfield," while various state delegations took their banners and surrounded the Ohioan. Order could not be restored for a full thirty
minutes. When the final vote was announced—Garfield, 399; Grant,
306; Blaine, 42; Sherman, 3—it was evident that one group, the
Stalwarts, remained defiant in their losing cause. Conkling rose to
make the nomination unanimous, but without uttering a single
compliment to Garfield. The New Yorker was said to be filled with
disgust at the outcome and considered Garfield unelectable.
Garfield, astonished at the week's events, wired Lucretia, who was
at the Mentor farm, "If the result meets your approval, I shall be
content."[15] Probably no Republican was more intrigued with the
convention's outcome than Hayes. "Garfield's nomination at Chicago was the best that was possible," said the outgoing president.
"He is the ideal candidate because he is the ideal self-made man."[16]

In choosing a vice presidential candidate, an effort was made to
appease the Stalwarts. Chester Alan Arthur, a Conkling confidant
and small-time Manhattan politician, who had been collector of
customs of the Port of New York—this position was the most prestigious and financially rewarding of all federal patronage jobs—
received the nod. And yet Conkling was said not to be placated.
Stories began to circulate that he had demanded Arthur turn down
the offer. Arthur supposedly refused his mentor's entreaties and
was purported to have told Conkling that he considered it a
tremendous honor to be nominated for the vice presidency and one
that, considering his less than exalted position in American politics,
would unlikely come his way again. Garfield's involvement in
choosing Arthur as his running mate is a matter of conjecture.
However, two things are certain: Garfield barely knew Arthur personally and did not agree with his politics.

Once the convention adjourned, Garfield was left with the
tricky task of mending the Republican Party's divisions, especially
Conkling's distrust of him. This had to be done expeditiously
because, as Garfield's campaign managers knew, he had little
chance of gaining the presidency without New York's electoral

votes. They decided to utilize the letter of acceptance—a practice of the time in which a presidential candidate elaborated upon his party's platform and clarified certain concerns of the day—to address the spoils system in American politics.

Pressure to reform the spoils system—its name derived from a quote by a U.S. senator in 1831 that "to the victor belong the spoils of the enemy"—began in 1871, when Congress authorized the Grant administration to set regulations for admission to public service and to appoint an oversight body, the Civil Service Commission.[17] This rudimentary merit system came to an inglorious end four years later due to funding problems. Nevertheless, the brief experiment proved that the merit system of civil service appointments could work well. When Hayes began to use competitive examinations as a basis for some of his political appointments, the boss-backed Stalwarts opposed the president's initiatives, arguing that it was an attempt to undo the state patronage systems they controlled. This line of reasoning was understandable because the financial stakes and political implications were enormous. For instance, Chester Arthur's post as collector of customs of the Port of New York produced an astonishing $100 million yearly in duties for federal coffers. The job itself, plus its de rigueur kickbacks, came with an annual salary of over $50,000—at a time when the average worker made less than $2,000 per year—and the port director oversaw a staff with combined incomes of $2 million. Conkling masterminded not only the appointments to the customs port but tens of thousands of other New York–based federal employees, including those along the Erie Canal. His financial empire was further buttressed by a requirement that each of these workers reimburse the New York State Republican Party 3 percent of their salary, in addition to special assessments that coincided with important elections.

Knowing that he had to conciliate Conkling and the Stalwarts, Garfield, the party loyalist, used his letter of acceptance to reject Hayes's growing use of nonpartisanship in filling government jobs and decried further attempts to reform the spoils system. "To select wisely from our vast population those who are best fitted for the many offices to be filled, requires an acquaintance far beyond the range of any one man," wrote Garfield. "The Executive should, therefore, seek and receive the information and assistance of those whose knowledge of the communities in which the duties are to be performed best qualifies them to aid in making the wisest choice."[18] Even with its concessions to the Stalwarts, and Garfield's acknowledgment that he would look to local officials to fill patronage positions, Conkling and his minions considered the letter's language to be too noncommittal to gain their support.

Garfield's managers suggested that he further placate Conkling by traveling to New York City for a one-on-one visit. At first, Garfield resisted the idea, but when his advisers told him that there would be serious trouble in managing the campaign if he did not agree to such a meeting, there was little else to do. "I am very reluctant to go," Garfield confided in his diary. "It is an unreasonable demand that so much effort should be made to conciliate one man. But to resist the opinion of the whole Committee would be ungracious, and perhaps unwise."[19] A trip east did have its political downside. Garfield's reputation would suffer if the voters thought he was politically weak and forced to pay an embarrassing tribute to New York's Republican boss. To protect Garfield's image, a conference of leading Republicans was organized to coincide with the visit. Billed as a show of party unity to discuss campaign issues, the sham summit served to cover up the real intention of Garfield's stopover.

In an era when tradition dictated that presidential candidates do little actual campaigning, Garfield's two-day trip east included more than twenty-five railroad-car platform appearances. From Buffalo to Schenectady—the site of Arthur's alma mater, Union College—and on to New York City, enthusiastic crowds, some as large as 50,000 people, greeted him. Between towns, Garfield conducted informal receptions with local officials and politicians. In Manhattan, the sidewalks around Grand Central Depot were lined with well-wishers hoping to get a glimpse of the nominee. Whisked downtown to Twenty-third Street, Garfield was greeted by cheers as he walked into the Fifth Avenue Hotel. Throughout the night, hundreds of visitors crowded into his room.

The next day began with a surprise when Conkling disappeared. He was seen the night before checking into the hotel, but was not present for any of the meetings between Garfield and New York's Stalwarts. Conkling's friends, including Arthur, were embarrassed by his behavior, but there was little they could say. They understood that this was Conkling's inept way to make future denials. A century and a quarter after the event, historians still do not know what deals, if any, were struck. None of the participants left detailed accounts of the conversations. When he arrived back in Mentor, Garfield confided in his diary, "Very weary but feeling that no serious mistake had been made and probably much good had been done. No trades, no shackles, and as well fitted for defeat or victory as ever."[20] Several days later, Conkling reappeared and told anyone who would listen how Garfield had been humbled and that the nominee had made important concessions to the Stalwarts. With his ego apparently satisfied, Conkling grudgingly declared that he was ready to participate in the campaign.

The presidential campaign of 1880 was a hard-fought contest, full of personal attacks and bitter recriminations. Winfield S. Hancock, a renowned Civil War general and one of the architects of the North's triumph at Gettysburg, emerged as the Democrats' choice for president. No longer the physically dashing battlefield commander—in middle age, Hancock had ballooned to more than three hundred pounds—his nomination was as much a surprise to the Democrats as Garfield's was to the Republicans. Indeed, Hancock had little experience in civilian life and rarely appeared in public. But the fact that he lived in New York and had no political record to defend—he was commander of an army administrative center located on Governor's Island in the middle of New York Harbor— led the Democrats to believe that they could carry the state. The Democrats felt emboldened to attack Garfield's personal character and congressional record unmercifully.

The negative campaigning subjected Garfield to violent personal abuse, initially focused on his supposed perjury during the Crédit Mobilier affair. His moral fitness was questioned as Democrats alleged that he had received $329 as a dividend on his ten shares of Crédit Mobilier stock. The figure "329" became a rallying cry for the Democrats, who made certain it was prominently printed in newspapers or chalked on buildings, doorsteps, fences, and sidewalks. The Republican faithful, in a show of mocking disdain, began to wear their own "329" badges, intending to emphasize their candidate's three years in the Union army, two years in the Ohio senate, and nine terms in Congress. New Democratic charges seemed to be leveled on an almost daily basis and eventually included the hypocrisy of the "salary grab" of 1873 and corruption surrounding the DeGolyer-McClelland contract payments. One newspaper even assailed Garfield for having abandoned the army in 1863, claiming that his exchange of military camp life for a comfortable seat in Congress was cowardly.

Most of the charges against Garfield caused little political damage, and abiding by political convention—it was considered undignified and strategically unsound for a presidential candidate to speak at length at personal appearances—he remained ensconced at the family farm. "While I do not shrink from any attack or from any defense necessary to be made," Garfield wrote to a friend, "I think that the Democrats are feeling the force and pressure of the tide that is now sweeping against them. They dare not meet the issues raised . . . but are seeking to draw us off into personal controversy."[21]

Two weeks before the election, Republican optimism was suddenly muted when the *Truth*, an obscure New York City labor scandal sheet, published a letter, supposedly written by Garfield to an H. L. Morey of Lynn, Massachusetts, that called for unrestricted Chinese immigration and the right of a corporation to hire the cheapest labor available. The Morey letter came at a time when America's politicians had begun to effectively exploit anti-Chinese sentiment, particularly among voters in California. Immigration politics was volatile enough that both the Republican and Democratic Party platforms endorsed restrictions on Chinese immigration. Garfield even commented on the issue in his letter of acceptance. "[Chinese immigration] is too much like an importation to be welcomed without restriction; too much like an invasion to be looked upon without solicitude," he wrote. "We cannot consent to allow any form of servile labor to be introduced among us under the guise of immigration."[22] If the Morey letter was authentic, then Garfield would be revealed as a fraud and a hypocrite.

The Democrats wasted no time circulating the letter to major newspapers and posting copies of it in cities and villages throughout the country. Writing experts scrutinized the original and within days Garfield issued a handwritten statement condemning the Morey missive. Newspapers reprinted the two letters side by side so that readers could compare the handwriting for themselves. The controversy was finally settled when inspection revealed the handwritings to be different. In addition, the Morey letter contained numerous grammatical and spelling errors. Garfield, considered one of the most erudite men in American politics, justifiably claimed that he would never make such atrocious spelling mistakes. The Republicans launched investigations hoping to trace the letter back to the Democratic National Committee. The author was never conclusively identified, H. L. Morey could not be located, and the Democrats were forced to admit that the letter was an apparent forgery.

As a politician who excelled at speechmaking, Garfield found it difficult to remain in Mentor and not engage in active campaigning. He was, however, not isolated on the farm. A one-room outbuilding was remade into a campaign office and connected by telegraph to the world outside. From September through Election Day, numerous delegations of voters traveled by rail to see and hear the nominee. One day would bring eighty Fisk Jubilee Singers; the next, four hundred members of the Young Men's First Voters Garfield and Arthur Club of Cleveland; soon followed by five hundred associates of the Lincoln Club of Indianapolis, wearing linen dusters and three-cornered straw hats. With the throngs assembled near the farmhouse, Garfield gave what became known as "front-porch" addresses, and shook thousands of hands. "With innumerable critics, watchful and eager to catch a phrase that might be turned into ridicule or odium, or a sentence that might be distorted to his own or the party's injury," wrote a historian, "Garfield did not halt nor trip in any one of his seventy speeches."[23]

Election Day was clear and bright across most of the country. More than nine million individuals went to the polls and Garfield received a plurality of fewer than 2,000 votes—the closest popular vote in all presidential elections in American history. The electoral vote was less narrow, 214 to 155, with New York's 35 electoral votes proving crucial to the Garfield victory. He won New York by just 20,000 votes out of 1.1 million cast, and some observers attributed this margin of victory to switched votes by New York Democrats disgusted with their party's participation in the Morey debacle. In this first post-Reconstruction presidential election, the Democrats carried the entire South (thus establishing the tradition of the solid Democratic South), but Hancock won only four other states. Despite all the campaign controversies, Garfield proved to be a strong national candidate as Republicans regained control of the House of Representatives and forced a deadlock in the Senate, with tie votes to be decided by the new Republican vice president. Most observers agreed that, in view of the nastiness of the campaign, Garfield's victory could be regarded as a personal triumph. He had captured the presidency by keeping his party's faithful focused and united while presenting a positive and modest image to America's voters.

The day following the election, more than 500 letters and 150 telegrams of congratulations arrived in Mentor. President Hayes and his wife visited along with the president of Oberlin College and seventy students. It was an exciting time for Garfield—he was simultaneously a member of the House of Representatives, a United States senator-elect, and president-elect of the United States, the only instance this has occurred in history—but there was a sobering realization of how the win would affect him and his family. "I am not elated over the election," he wrote to a friend. "On the contrary, while appreciating the honor and the opportunities, I feel keenly the loss of liberty which accompanies it, and especially that it will in a great measure stop my growth."[24] New problems confronted Garfield, not the least of which were growing threats to his safety and the maddening claims of office seekers. Sherman forwarded a letter expressing concern that, in view of the bitterness of the politics of the day, Garfield could be the target of an assassination plot. Garfield replied that he did not consider such danger to be a problem. Telling Sherman that he had already received a number of threatening letters, Garfield reminded him, "Assassination can be no more guarded against than death by lightning; and it is best not to worry about either."[25]

6

Garfield's Administration

From the time of the election through his inauguration on March 4, 1881, Garfield was embroiled in political haggling over the formation of his cabinet. This wrangling was fueled by concerns of Garfield's friends and foes that his kindhearted nature would yield to all sorts of pressure, leaving him at the mercy of certain Republican factions. Even more troubling was the possibility that a new cabinet officer might take advantage of Garfield's trust and use his position to further his own presidential ambitions. In public, Garfield was silent about the negotiations, but in private, the talks degenerated into a diplomatic row involving himself, Blaine, and Conkling.

Early on, Garfield decided to offer the secretary of state post to Blaine. This appointment was traditionally the most prestigious of administration positions. Foreign governments considered the secretary of state to be the American president's prime minister, and, even in the United States, the secretary of state was considered more influential than the vice president or other cabinet members. In late November, during a weeklong visit to Washington, Garfield breakfasted with Blaine and provisionally offered him the top post in the cabinet. It was an interesting choice considering that only one year before, Garfield had written that he was wary of Blaine's shrewdness. "There is an element in him that I distrust," Garfield

said of Blaine. He is "a brilliant, aggressive, [but] calculating man."[1]
Garfield's opinion changed during the course of the convention and
the campaign, and he now considered Blaine to be "the prince of
good fellows."[2] Much of the goodwill stemmed from Garfield's
recognition of Blaine's preeminent position in the party, and how
Blaine and his Half-Breed followers had shifted their support to
Garfield at a crucial time during the nominating convention. At the
breakfast meeting, Blaine assured Garfield that he had no plans to
run again for the presidency and would work harmoniously with
whomever else was in the administration.

Garfield returned to Mentor hoping that Republican infighting
would lessen, but this was not the case. He was soon inundated
with advice from Blaine, most of it describing the current state of
the party and how to deal with the various bosses, especially Conkling. "Of course it would not be wise to make war on them. Indeed,
that would be folly," wrote Blaine. "They must not be knocked
down with bludgeons: they must have their throats cut with a
feather."[3] Blaine might have agreed to curtail his presidential aspirations, but his impulse to take over a situation remained. More
important, his analysis of the Republicans' state of affairs conve-
niently neglected that it was Conkling and his Stalwarts who could
justifiably claim some credit for Garfield's win in New York and
ultimately the presidency. The fact that Garfield's replies were generally noncommittal and never disputed Blaine's conjectures—in
one of his letters, Garfield wrote to Blaine, "our friendship . . . tested
in so many ways, gives assurance that we can happily unite in working out the important problems which confront us"—probably led
the secretary of state–designate to believe that he would be the piv-
otal politician in the new administration.[4]

Despite intentions to keep Blaine's appointment secret, word
was leaked and the Stalwarts were furious. Conkling demanded
that the other high-ranking cabinet post, secretary of the Treasury,
be reserved for one of his men. Since the Treasury secretary controlled a vast amount of federal patronage, in addition to supervis-
ing the all-important monetary policies of the nation, Conkling saw

untold opportunities. The difficulty arose because Garfield let it be known that he regarded an easterner, especially one from New York where the country's financial power was concentrated, an inappropriate choice. The Stalwarts realized that much of Garfield's thinking about the Treasury position was influenced by Blaine. "Your secretary of the treasury should be taken from the West," Blaine wrote Garfield in mid-December. "This is so evident that I do not stop to argue. He must be identified with an agricultural community, not a manufacturing or commercial community."[5]

Conkling dispatched several of his subordinates to Mentor, with the hope of persuading Garfield to change his attitude. Garfield began by telling his guests that "it would be most unwise in a party sense to give the place to N.Y. City." When one of the New Yorkers said that Conkling hoped to "sustain" the new administration, Garfield took it as political blackmail. "I answered," Garfield wrote in his diary, that "I would not permit this four years to be used to secure the next for anybody."[6] Matters worsened a few weeks later, when Blaine composed an editorial for the *New York Tribune*, prefaced with the words "by authority": "The incoming administration will see to it that the men from New York and from the other states, who had the courage at Chicago to obey the wishes of their districts in the balloting for president and who thus finally voted for Garfield shall not lose by it," intoned Blaine. "The administration . . . will not permit its friends to be persecuted for their friendship."[7] The Stalwarts interpreted this as sentiments coming directly from Garfield.

The editorial infuriated Conkling, who thought that Blaine had gained complete control over Garfield's policies. Although Garfield had not authorized Blaine to write the article, he did nothing to repudiate it. Blaine, in his furtive way, was accomplishing exactly what the New York Stalwarts feared: he would prevent them from being appointed to high-level cabinet positions. When Garfield asked whether a reconciliation might be brought about by inviting Conkling into the cabinet, a stunned Blaine cautioned Garfield, "His appointment would act like strychnine upon your administration—

first, bring contortions and then be followed by death."[8] For two dispiriting months, Garfield drew up constantly changing cabinet slates, all of which were commented on by Blaine. None passed muster, and when the Garfield family left Mentor in late February for the inauguration, the president-elect had numerous alternatives but no firm commitments other than from Blaine.

The intense politicking and emphasis on personality that so engaged Blaine and Conkling held little appeal for Garfield. "I regret that I have so little time to feed myself on the beauties which the Season spreads over the world," Garfield confided in his diary. "I must shut myself up to the study of man's estimate of himself as contrasted with my own estimate of him."[9] It was this loss of personal freedom, time away from books, family, and a growing sense of intellectual isolation, that most troubled Garfield. The days prior to the inauguration should have been filled with excitement but, once in Washington, Garfield's hours consisted of irksome negotiating over the cabinet selections. Newspapers played up the discord, particularly the dealings with Conkling, but most of the reporting was inaccurate gossip and innuendo. Whether Garfield could equally recognize both the Stalwarts and the Half-Breeds, without antagonizing the other, remained questionable.

Attempting to strike a political and geographical balance, Garfield asked Robert Todd Lincoln, the son of President Lincoln, to become secretary of war. This appointment pleased most Republicans, especially the bosses from Illinois, and brought an undeniable luster to the cabinet. From Pennsylvania, Garfield chose Isaac MacVeagh to be attorney general. Although an independent-minded Republican, MacVeagh was the son-in-law of the Stalwart-leaning boss of the state. Representing the West, Senator Samuel Kirkwood was named secretary of the interior. Held in high regard by Garfield, the aged Kirkwood had gained a reputation as a hard-nosed Republican battling antiwar Democratic "Copperheads" when he was governor of Iowa.

Attempting to mollify Conkling, Garfield offered one of the New York Stalwarts the post of secretary of the navy. As with every proposition that Garfield put forth, it was taken as a political insult and answered with a sharp rebuke. Switching strategies, Garfield named William Hunt, a lawyer living in Louisiana, to that position. Refusing to listen any further to Conkling's entreaties concerning the Treasury slot, Garfield filled the office with William Windom of Minnesota, who, as chairman of the Senate's Appropriations Committee, had a practical knowledge of the nation's finances. One cabinet position was left, postmaster general, and attempts to fill the slot prompted another volley of abuse from Conkling.

Hoping to have some representation by the New York Stalwart faction in his cabinet, Garfield asked Thomas James to be postmaster general. James, the postmaster of New York City, directed his job with uncommon efficiency and received plaudits for his managerial skills. Despite being Conkling's close friend, James was described by Garfield as "free and earnest," and, when offered the position, James accepted on the spot.[10] But to choose a follower of Conkling, without first discussing the situation with him, was considered a breach of political etiquette greater even than to appoint one of Conkling's foes. So upset was Conkling about the James appointment that he and vice president–elect Arthur paid an unannounced visit to Garfield. For over an hour, Conkling browbeat Garfield, charging him with duplicity and lack of concern for the needs of the Republican Party. Arthur recalled that "for invective, sarcasm, and impassioned eloquence, this was the speech of Conkling's life."[11] Garfield listened to the harangue in silence. He made no promises and gave no apologies, but came away convinced, more than ever, that Conkling had little regard for most of his fellow Republicans.

For Garfield, the dreary ordeal of choosing a cabinet was complete. "The result is better than I expected," he wrote in his diary. "Though not an ideal cabinet, it is a good combination of *esse et videri* [to be and to seem]."[12] Garfield's critics were not so certain. Some suggested it was a volatile combination of Republican factions that would result in endless conflict. Others called the cabinet strictly a Blaine affair with Garfield coerced into being Blaine's private secretary and the members a "board of recording scribes."[13] Certain observers viewed it as lacking any Conkling representation, noting that without his backing little would be accomplished. Indeed, it was none of these. Garfield managed, under difficult circumstances, to assemble a cabinet that reflected his patient and unthreatening style of leadership. No one privy to all the private discussions could say that Garfield's selection had been imposed on him by any single Republican boss or faction. Certainly, Blaine's influence was substantive and Conkling's attitude was dismissive, but Garfield's choices were as good a start for the administration as could be anticipated.

Friday, March 4, dawned snowy and gloomy. Garfield, who had been working on his inaugural speech until almost three A.M., was exhausted as he prepared for what should have been one of the most exciting days of his life. Writing the inaugural address had proven more difficult and tiresome than he had anticipated. Around Christmastime, Garfield first began to read the speeches of his predecessors. Adams's was better than Washington's, but Garfield considered it too lengthy. Jefferson spoke too ornately and used "unnecessary self-depreciating" comments.[14] Madison's words did not match Garfield's expectations. Monroe's address, however, was better than he anticipated, particularly the section detailing the history of American independence. Despite his readings, Garfield was preoccupied with the process of selecting a cabinet and, less than a month before inauguration day, he entertained the possibility of not giving a speech. "It is difficult to understand the singular repugnance I feel in regard to doing this work," he wrote in his diary.[15] Not until the middle of February would Garfield make any progress on the talk.

By noon, snow was no longer falling as Hayes, Garfield, and their wives rode up Pennsylvania Avenue in an open barouche drawn by four horses. The regally dressed First Cleveland Troop marched before them as an honor guard. Among those waiting at the Capitol building were the Garfield children, numerous members of the extended family, and Eliza, Garfield's mother. She would be the first

woman in American history to witness her son's inauguration as
president. Garfield looked weary, the effect of sleepless nights and
anxiety over his cabinet selections clearly visible on his face. The
inaugural address lasted thirty-five minutes and, according to one
Garfield biographer, was that "of a tired man, entirely unworthy of
the high reputation that Garfield had justly earned as one of the
most effective American orators."[16] Garfield's voice was hoarse and
his dramatic and exuberant body language, which he had used so
effectively throughout his career, was absent.

Considering his intellectualism and erudite ways, Garfield's inaugural address was remarkable for being unremarkable. There
were no memorable passages or great ringing phrases. "We stand
today upon an eminence which overlooks a hundred years of
national life," it began, "a century crowded with perils, but crowned
with triumphs of liberty and love."[17] For the first several minutes,
he blandly chronicled the history of the nation and the importance
of the Civil War in bringing about societal shifts from which there
was no turning back. "The elevation of the Negro race from slavery
to full rights of citizenship, is the most important political change
we have known since the adoption of the Constitution of 1776," he
proclaimed. "So far as my authority can lawfully extend, they shall
enjoy full and equal protection of the Constitution and laws."[18] He
acknowledged that many issues arising from emancipation had yet
to be resolved, but provided few answers. Education ("the saving
influence of universal education"), finances ("the refunding of the
national debt at a low rate of interest should be accomplished"),
and religious freedom ("nor can any ecclesiastical organization be
safely permitted to usurp in the smallest degree the functions and
powers of the National Government") occupied the last half of the
talk.[19] When, in closing, Garfield briefly touched upon civil service
reform, the politicians stirred. But, like the words before it, Garfield
said little and promised even less.

Following the ceremonies at the Capitol, there was a traditional
military parade of over 15,000 men. Immediately after reviewing
the procession, an emotional Garfield entertained members of the

Williams College Alumni Association, including Mark Hopkins, his now elderly mentor. The festivities ended with a sumptuous "Inaugural Reception and Promenade Concert" at the National Museum, with music by the Marine Band of John Philip Sousa, and a magnificent display of fireworks. It was after eleven o'clock when the Garfields returned to the White House, their expected home for the next four years. An exhausted Garfield did not go to bed until nearly one A.M.

In the morning, after little more than five hours of sleep, Garfield stopped in the downstairs public rooms of the White House. There he was greeted by hundreds of people, and prevalent among them was, according to his description, "the indurated office seeker who pursues his prey with the grip of death."[20] In 1881, government job seekers enjoyed open access to the executive mansion, and it was not uncommon that they attempted to speak one-on-one with the president to plead their case. Such encounters became distracting to Garfield, and he increasingly relied on secretarial clerks to handle the throngs. Despite the daily chaos that office seekers created, Garfield rejected the idea of positioning armed guards at the doors of the White House. So loosely monitored was the White House that, when Saturday afternoon receptions were held, the general public was allowed to go through the receiving line with no questions asked. High government officials freely mingled with average citizens and security was not a major concern.

During one of Garfield's first forays into the East Room, he was, as expected, surrounded by crowds of office seekers thrusting résumés and other personal papers into his hands. One of the documents was a copy of a short speech, "Garfield against Hancock," on which, boldly written in pencil, were the words "Paris Consulship" connected by a drawn line to the author's name, Charles Julius Guiteau.[21] He was a short, scrawny forty-year-old, who, although a self-educated lawyer, fancied himself more a world-class theologian and novelist. Indeed, he was nothing of the sort. Guiteau was a mentally unstable, penny-ante scalawag, who stole from everyone he knew. He was the child of a deceased schizophrenic mother and a religion-obsessed, know-it-all father. Following the 1880 presidential political campaign, Guiteau became fixated on the belief that the efforts he had made to elect Garfield should be rewarded by a top patronage appointment to the consulship in Paris or the mission in Vienna. Guiteau's campaign efforts, however, consisted of little more than giving an incoherent speech of meaningless clichés to whomever would listen to him on a New York City street corner.

Several weeks later, during one of the Garfields' Saturday general receptions in April, Guiteau cornered Lucretia and presented her with his calling card. He engaged the First Lady in small talk, telling her that he was one of the men who had made her husband president. She smiled and chatted for a while, and then went on to greet the next person in the crowd of visitors. Guiteau made it a point to attend the White House receptions as a way of keeping his name in the minds of the clerks there. He had done the same with officials in the State Department, who regarded Guiteau as more of a nuisance then a bona fide office seeker. Eventually, he became enough of a pest that Blaine, who knew Guiteau by sight and name, told him to stop bothering the State Department secretaries. "I told him," recalled Blaine, "that there was no prospect whatever of his receiving the appointments, and that I did not want him to continue his visits: I wanted to bring them to an end."[22] Guiteau grew so demanding in his insistence on obtaining the Paris appointment that by June he was similarly barred from entering the White House.

Contending with the onslaught of office seekers, as well as juggling the political wishes of the Half-Breeds and Stalwarts, consumed much of Garfield's time. But, even during these days of public harassment and political deadlock, Garfield, through his cabinet officials, worked on other issues of national and international importance. Garfield sent Secretary of the Treasury Windom and Attorney General MacVeagh to speak with Wall Street bankers and brokers to devise a method to redeem 5 and 6 percent government bonds, mostly used to finance public debt dating from the Civil

War, in favor of the new 3½ percent bonds. "It would be a very brilliant feat of financiering," Garfield wrote in his diary.[23] Agreeing with Windom's and MacVeagh's reasoning, the Wall Streeters worked out an ingenious system to redeem the old bonds and replace them with new ones while not substantively affecting the original bondholders' financial stake. With successful completion of the refinancing, Garfield's administration succeeded in reducing interest on the public debt by over 40 percent, an annual savings to the United States Treasury of more than $10 million. Not only were the country's monetary underpinnings strengthened, but Windom's and MacVeagh's reputations were enhanced. This was important because Blaine had argued against their cabinet appointments, and Windom's and MacVeagh's new stature provided an important counterbalance to Blaine's bullying.

Despite his preoccupation with domestic political affairs, Blaine's grasp of international developments was matched by few other individuals in government. He was particularly interested in protecting the United States' interests in the Caribbean and Central and South America, a subject that Garfield had mentioned in his inaugural address. "Blaine read an important note to several of our leading Ministers in Europe on the neutrality of the South American Isthmus," wrote Garfield about one cabinet meeting, "holding that the U.S. has guaranteed its neutrality and denies the right of other, especially European, powers to take any part in the guarantee."[24] But it was not just this restating of the Monroe Doctrine that so interested both Garfield and Blaine; they were the first president and secretary of state to consider the United States as an emerging two-ocean power. Not only did Garfield proclaim American sovereignty over any canal that might be built on the Central American isthmus, he also viewed the Hawaiian Islands as an extension of the country's Pacific coastline. Realizing that control of the islands would be integral to the country's western growth, Garfield asked one of his most trusted childhood friends to assume the position of minister to Hawaii. "The condition of the Hawaiian kingdom is such as to give us a good deal of anxiety," Garfield wrote his associate. "The King has started on a voyage around the world, and it is feared he is contemplating either the sale of the Islands or some commercial treaty with Europeans powers which would embarrass the United States."[25] Telling his friend to begin diplomatic negotiation with the islands' king, Garfield signaled his intent to expand America's international hegemony. In European affairs, Garfield approved plans to have the United States join the Geneva Convention, which helped to establish the International Red Cross. Subsequently, he assisted in organizing this country's National Association of the Red Cross.

Garfield's interest in domestic financial issues led to an investigation that uncovered one of the celebrated scandals of late-nineteenth-century American politics: the U.S. Post Office's "Star Route fraud." Beginning with the Grant administration and through the Hayes presidency, there had been persistent rumors of corruption in the management of the national postal service. Congress had looked into the allegations, but nothing was done to correct the few abuses that were found. Alarmed that the new administration would be perceived as misusing Post Office funds, Blaine warned Garfield that the situation needed to be remedied. Blaine's admonition was partially based on his own belief that Conkling's forces were somehow involved in the dishonesty. Blaine's advice was timely—although his impression concerning Conkling's participation was incorrect—since over the prior two years the postal service had run up annual deficits of more than $1 million, most of which were covered by special congressional appropriations. Detailed analysis of the shortfall indicated that it was mostly due to the unanticipated and exorbitant cost of delivering mail in certain poorly populated regions of the Southwest. Because these districts were considered special mail routes, they were designated by an asterisk or star on printed postal schedules. Financial outrage developed because the delivery fees were fraudulently increased by tens of thousands of dollars to provide supposedly expedited service to each of ninety-three selected star routes. In one well-publicized example, a single route cost the government $50,000 a year for speeded-up service—

the original contract called for an expenditure of approximately $1,000—even though no letter or newspaper had been delivered for a period of a month and a half. Investigators knew that such widespread fraud could occur only with the consent of highly placed officials within the Post Office and other areas of the government.

Five days after his inauguration, Garfield discussed the Star Route situation with Postmaster General James. Told to investigate any misdeeds, James enlisted the assistance of Attorney General MacVeagh, and, within several weeks, they had uncovered enough information to alert Garfield that he was facing a scandal of enormous magnitude. James and MacVeagh discovered that the two main suspects were Garfield's presidential campaign manager and his primary fund-raiser. According to eyewitness accounts, Garfield walked across the room, reflected on the situation, and said, "Go ahead regardless of where or whom you hit. I direct you not only to probe this ulcer to the bottom, but to cut it out."[26] Within three months, expenses for the ninety-three Star Routes were reduced by almost $800,000 per year. James and MacVeagh delved further into the fraud and the Star Route scandal, and its congressional probes, indictments, jury tamperings, trials, and mistrials would occupy the front pages of America's newspapers long after Garfield's death.

As the Star Route scandal widened, the ongoing patronage controversy with Conkling also increased in intensity and entered a new and, for Garfield, politically risky phase. In mid-March, Garfield invited Conkling to spend a Sunday afternoon at the White House to privately discuss appointments in New York. Garfield agreed with many of Conkling's suggestions, but remarked that he also needed to recognize some of the New York men who had supported him in Chicago. In the New York delegation at the nominating convention, twenty men, organized around state senator William H. Robertson, had refused Conkling's wishes to support Grant through the unit rule. This group had supported Blaine for thirty-five ballots and then switched to Garfield on the thirty-sixth. Neither Stalwart nor Half-Breed, these individuals were termed Independents or Reformers, and Conkling did not want any of them, particularly Robertson, appointed to important posts in the government. Indeed, Conkling told Garfield they were worthy only of foreign assignments. "I said they did not deserve exile, but rather a place in the affairs of their own state," Garfield wrote in his diary. "I will go as far as I can to keep the peace; but I will not abandon the N.Y. protestants."[27]

A few days later, Garfield sent to the Senate a number of nominations for New York patronage positions. All of the names were followers of Conkling; the Independents received no offers. Garfield's allies were alarmed that he had capitulated to Conkling and surrendered all federal patronage in the state to the Stalwarts. One historian wrote of the Garfield-Conkling relationship, "It is almost pathetic to see how persistently Garfield clung to his hope of coming to a good friendly understanding with Conkling and thereby ending all troubles, when not a trace of any such feeling appears in anything reported from the other side."[28] Such a strategy might have been in Garfield's mind, but that evening an irate Blaine rushed to the White House to change Garfield's thinking.

Blaine was dissatisfied over the naming of Conkling's followers and, during the course of two hours, managed to convince Garfield that the situation needed immediate rectification. "I have broken Blaine's heart with the appointments I have made today," Garfield told Lucretia. "He regards me as having surrendered to Conkling. I have not, but I don't know but that I have acted too hastily."[29] The next morning—whether he discussed his plans with Blaine or anyone else remains historical conjecture—Garfield sent to the Senate the nomination of Robertson as collector of customs of the Port of New York. To appoint one of Conkling's enemies to the most coveted of all patronage positions was both a bold political stroke and a supreme insult to the Stalwarts. "This brings on the contest at once and will settle the question whether the President is registering clerk of the Senate or the Executive of the United States," Garfield wrote to one of his friends. "Shall the principal port of entry in which more than 90% of all our customs duties are collected be under the control of the administration or under the local control of a factional senator."[30]

As Garfield asserted his independence from the Republican senatorial bosses, an enraged Conkling sent James and MacVeagh to the White House to discuss the situation. The two cabinet members, under pressure from Conkling, told Garfield that they felt compelled to resign. Garfield assured them they were too important to the welfare of the nation to become embroiled in the political affairs of a single state. James and MacVeagh reneged on their pledge to Conkling and agreed to remain in the cabinet. The Robertson affair remained unresolved for several weeks because the Senate was in the process of organizing its various committees. During this time, the battle of wills between Garfield and Conkling became daily news, with every detail of the dispute displayed as front-page headlines. Garfield came under intense pressure to recall the Robertson nomination, but he remained steadfast in his desire to humble Conkling and defeat the practice of boss rule.

The political standoff was further swayed by Garfield's hostile relationship with his vice president, Chester Arthur. In an era when running mates did not necessarily espouse similar points of view, Garfield and Arthur were the bitterest of rivals, unhappily brought together by the vagaries of Republican infighting. As one of Conkling's confidants, Arthur was so incensed about the Robertson situation that for several weeks he refused to speak to Garfield. Almost one month later, Arthur deigned to meet with the president, and curtly told him the Robertson nomination would inevitably cause the downfall of the Republicans in New York. "Yes, it will defeat us if the leaders [Conkling and you] determine it shall," retorted Garfield.[31] Garfield hoped that Arthur would demonstrate some political politesse but this never occurred. Matters got further out of hand when Arthur began to call the president a liar. "Garfield has not been square, nor honorable, nor truthful," Arthur told the editor of the *New York Herald*. "It is a hard thing to say of a President of the United States, but it is, unfortunately, only the truth."[32] Garfield was furious over Arthur's name-calling and asked that the vice president be barred from the White House.

Despite the political nastiness, public opinion ran increasingly in Garfield's favor, and, as soon as Conkling realized that Robertson's nomination would be passed by his fellow senators, he took drastic action. Conkling resigned from the Senate, confident that the New York State legislature would vindicate him with speedy reelection. With refreshed backing, Conkling thought he would be able to humiliate Garfield and control the Republicans' future legislative calendar. "Conkling, who has always inclined to think someone was trying to 'humiliate' him, has succeeded in inflicting measureless humiliation on himself," wrote an ecstatic Garfield. "Suicide is the chief mode of political death after all."[33] Two days after the histrionic resignation of Conkling, Robertson was confirmed by a voice vote of the Senate. Garfield noted in his diary, "This is a great relief."[34]

Garfield's strength of purpose brought him much acclaim. "He has risen immensely in popular estimation," wrote one of Garfield's friends, "and got credit for a back-bone he was never thought by the masses to possess."[35] Not only did Garfield receive admiring notice from the public, but the New York legislature backed his stand against bossism when word went out to Conkling that his unorthodox scheme would probably not get him reelected. Conkling's supporters were clearly angered, but for one of his enthusiasts it turned into a good deal more than mere resentment. Beginning in April and extending through June, Charles Guiteau wrote a series of letters to Garfield condemning Robertson and urging the appointment of a Stalwart in his place. Guiteau was a voracious reader of newspapers, especially the anti-Garfield *New York Herald* and the Washington-based *National Republican*. His fears about the wickedness of Garfield and Blaine, and how they were dividing the country and destroying Republican Party harmony, were reinforced on a daily basis. In Guiteau's disturbed mind, Garfield was a traitor to the Republican cause. Guiteau believed that a strong Stalwart faction was the country's only safeguard against the Democrats assuming control and forcing the start of another civil war.

Several days after Conkling's mid-May resignation from the Senate, Guiteau decided that Garfield needed to be removed from office. "The more I read, the more I saw the complication of public affairs," he said. "I kept reading the papers and kept being impressed, and the idea kept bearing and bearing and bearing down upon me."[36] By early June, Guiteau convinced himself that eliminating Garfield was the will of God and that he was God's executioner. To carry out his mission, Guiteau purchased a .44-caliber snub-nosed revolver, nicknamed the British Bull Dog for its destructive power. Guiteau was so convinced of the righteousness of his actions that the gun he selected was an upgraded model with an inlaid ivory grip. He reasoned that Americans would consider him a hero, and the pistol used to kill Garfield should be elegant in appearance since it would be placed on permanent display in Washington.

Guiteau was obsessed with his undertaking. Numerous times he went down to the Potomac River flats to practice firing the weapon. He wrote a lengthy letter explaining his actions, to be published at the time of the shooting. And he began to stalk the president. First, he simply watched Garfield walk through Lafayette Square Park. Then, he followed him to the Disciples of Christ Church on Vermont Avenue, where he stood in the back, his revolver in his pocket, and noted where Garfield sat. The pastor gave what Garfield termed "a very stupid sermon on a very great subject," while an impatient Guiteau wildly shouted out non sequiturs to the congregation.[37] In his diary for that day, Garfield even mentioned the presence in the church of "a dull young man, with a loud voice, trying to pound noise into the question 'What think ye of Christ?' "[38] After the service was over, Guiteau walked outside of the church to a window near Garfield's pew to determine whether a shot through it would be possible. Satisfied that the church would be an ideal place to kill Garfield, Guiteau decided on the next Sunday, June 19, as the perfect day for a political murder.

Continuing to scour the daily papers, Guiteau read of a change in Garfield's schedule. The president would not be attending church on the nineteenth. Instead, he and Lucretia were planning

to leave Washington on Saturday, the eighteenth, for a short recu-
peratory rest in Elberon, on the New Jersey shore. Garfield, weary
from the recent battle with Conkling and his Stalwarts, and Lucretia, recovering from a bout of malaria, looked forward to several
days in the salubrious ocean air. Lucretia's illness had been particularly severe and, for a time, there was a question of her survival. "My
anxiety for her dominates all my thoughts," confided Garfield in his
diary, "and makes me feel that I am fit for nothing."[39]

The Garfields were longtime proponents of homeopathic
healing—an alternative system of medical treatment based on the
theory that diseases can be cured by giving small doses of drugs that
produce, in a healthy person and in large doses, the symptoms
found in those who were sick. This premise became regarded as the
first law of homeopathy, derived from the Latin aphorism *similia
similibus curantur*, or like is cured by like (a sort of "fighting fire
with fire" therapy). In early May, when Lucretia's temperature
reached 104 degrees, Garfield arranged for one of her local doctors,
Susan Edson, a practitioner of homeopathy, to stay in the White
House. As Lucretia's condition worsened, Garfield sent for Jedediah Baxter, the army's chief medical purveyor and a respected
Washington nonhomeopathic physician, to consult. He agreed with
Edson's diagnosis of malaria, but thought that spinal meningitis
might be present as well. Leaving little to chance, Garfield summoned his relative and boyhood neighbor Silas Boynton—the same
cousin he had nearly killed forty years earlier by an accidental ax
blow—to travel to the executive mansion. Boynton, who lived in
Cleveland, was a renowned homeopathic doctor and the Garfield
family's longtime personal physician. Not until the end of May did
Lucretia's temperature finally return to near normal. It was Boynton who suggested that Lucretia's recovery would proceed faster in
the salty air of the seaside.

When the Garfields left for Elberon, Guiteau was waiting at the
train depot. Watching the president and Lucretia walk toward the
train, Guiteau changed his mind as he saw how sickly Lucretia
seemed. "Mrs. Garfield looked so thin, and she clung so tenderly to

the President's arm," according to Guiteau, "that I did not have the heart to fire on him."[40] On Monday, June 27, Garfield returned to Washington, having left Lucretia to continue her convalescence in Elberon. Guiteau, having carefully tracked Garfield's whereabouts, learned that the president was scheduled to return to New Jersey on Saturday morning, July 2.

For Garfield, the few days back in Washington allowed him to complete much of his official business as he prepared plans for an extended summer vacation, including attendance at the twenty-fifth reunion celebration of his graduation from Williams College. Last-minute meetings with most of his cabinet officers were scheduled, as well as discussions concerning the end of the 1880–81 fiscal year. Garfield dictated letters, appointed twenty-five foreign ministers and consuls, and named Blaine's son to be the third assistant secretary of state. On Friday night, July 1, Garfield walked alone to Blaine's house on Fifteenth Street. They talked about Conkling and how his fellow New York politicians were finally giving him his comeuppance. Garfield told Blaine that Vice President Arthur so annoyed him that he would continue his policy of not inviting him to the White House and, if forced to do so, that he wished Blaine would be there to serve as an intermediary. Arm-in-arm, a laughing Blaine escorted an ebullient Garfield back to Pennsylvania Avenue and assured him that in the morning he would accompany him to the train depot. Garfield had much to be satisfied with, not the least of which were the political triumphs of his new administration.

That same night, Guiteau inquired of the doorkeeper at the White House when Garfield would be departing in the morning. Given the information, Guiteau confirmed what he had read in the day's papers. Garfield was to board a 9:30 A.M. train at the Baltimore and Potomac depot. Retiring to his room at a boardinghouse, Guiteau wrote out one last explanation of his reasons for assassinating the president. He would give this letter to reporters to convince the nation of the righteousness of his actions.

7

The Assassination Attempt

The following morning, Blaine personally drove Garfield the few blocks to the Baltimore and Potomac train depot (on the current site of the National Gallery of Art). They chatted along the way and, at the station, remained in the carriage for a few more minutes of conversation as Blaine playfully tossed his cane in the air. Although he was not traveling northward with the president, Blaine wanted to go inside to say good-bye to the other cabinet officers and their wives, including Secretary of the Navy Hunt, Postmaster General James, Secretary of War Lincoln, and Secretary of the Treasury Windom, who were to accompany Garfield on his two-week vacation through New England. A now healthier Lucretia was taking a separate train from the New Jersey shore and was scheduled to join her husband in New York City.

At 9:20 A.M., Garfield and Blaine stepped out of the small coupe and, walking arm-in-arm, started toward the B Street (the nineteenth-century name for Constitution Avenue) entrance of the ladies' waiting room. Nearing the entryway, their arms separated as the president turned to ask a policeman how much time he had before the train departed. The officer told Garfield he had ten minutes. Blaine stepped slightly ahead of the president to allow him more room through the doorway. The waiting area was mostly deserted except for an on-duty female attendant, several passersby, and a down-and-out-looking man, who moved nervously about in the shadows of the room's main entrance. Once Garfield and Blaine, walking side by side with Garfield on the left, were halfway into the room, the stranger, having spotted the two top-hatted figures, moved toward them. When he was six feet behind and to the extreme right, the man drew a revolver from his coat, leveled it across his arm, and fired.

The shot passed through Garfield's right coat sleeve, causing a slight flesh wound of the upper arm. Some of the eyewitnesses thought a firecracker had been lit in honor of the president's departure. Garfield and Blaine flinched at the loud sound. Almost immediately, a second shot rang out and entered the middle of the right side of Garfield's back. As the president fell to the floor, he uttered several inaudible words. Instinctively, Blaine lunged toward the shooter, whom he recognized as Charles Guiteau, the odd office seeker from the State Department. Following Guiteau toward an exit, Blaine excitedly shouted, "Rockwell! Where is Rockwell?" as he looked for Garfield's personal assistant and longtime friend Almon Rockwell. Guiteau fled, but just as he was leaving the waiting area, he was apprehended by a ticket agent and the policeman who had spoken to Garfield just a moment before. Guiteau, still with the pistol in his hand, was quickly led away through an adjacent waiting salon, as he muttered, "I did it and will go to jail for it. I am a Stalwart and Arthur will be president."[1]

Back inside the ladies' waiting area, confusion reigned. Garfield lay helpless while his blood began to pool on the wooden boards. The woman in charge of the room rushed to cradle his head. Blaine turned back to find Garfield semiconscious. Quickly, onlookers gathered around the fallen president; some attempted to move him into a sitting position, others went to hold his hand, one bystander placed a wet handkerchief on his brow, but nobody seemed to know what to do. One hundred yards away, on the platform adjacent to the presidential train, but out of sight and earshot of the rapidly unfolding events in the depot's waiting area, the atmosphere was festive. Hunt and Windom smoked cigars while James and Lincoln spoke to fellow passengers and several accompanying reporters. They were all congratulating themselves on escaping Washington's hot weather. An employee of the Postal Railway Service excitedly ran toward James yelling that the president had been shot. "What!" exclaimed James. "There is no joke in a thing like that."[2] When told for a second time that it was true, the four cabinet officers sprinted back inside the station.

By this time, people were crowding into the ladies' waiting room. A distressed Blaine, crying out, "O my poor President!" tried to shield Garfield from the growing crowd.[3] Garfield's teenage sons, one in tears, were at their father's side. Windom lost control of his emotions and started to sob uncontrollably, while James bent down to assist Blaine. Lincoln and Hunt began to issue orders. Several railroad workers were sent to retrieve a coarse hay-and-horsehair mattress from an adjoining room. The still stuporous Garfield was rolled on to it. Suddenly, cries of "Lynch him! Hang him!" were heard from a gathering crowd outside as Guiteau, surrounded by a squad of policemen who had been summoned by telephone, was led away to police headquarters.[4] He frantically flourished a letter above his head, yelling out that the communiqué he had written would explain all.

Messengers were sent looking for any accessible physician. Within minutes, Smith Townshend, a health officer for the District of Columbia, arrived. He found a dazed Garfield with a nearly absent pulse. The physician told the onlookers that the president had fainted and instructed them to remove the wet cloth from his forehead and not sit him up but instead lower his head. Townshend asked someone in the crowd to fetch brandy from the depot's restaurant, and he instructed another person to obtain aromatic ammonia spirit (smelling salts) from a nearby apothecary shop. Mixing the two liquids together, Townshend helped a barely alert Garfield swallow the stimulant concoction. Garfield perked up and, when asked if he was in pain, told the doctor that his right leg and foot had a severe "prickling sensation." Turning Garfield on his side to examine the bullet hole, Townshend became the first of what would be numerous individuals to place their unwashed fingers and unclean instruments directly into the president's wound. "I did nothing further than to remove with my finger a small clot of blood from its mouth," Townshend innocently recalled. Garfield inquired about the injury and when Townshend told him it was not serious—Townshend lied, for he believed the wound was fatal—the president shook his head sideways, indicating that he disagreed with the doctor's assessment.

With the crowd pressing forward, Blaine, Townshend, and the other cabinet officers decided to move Garfield to a more private area. Several porters carried the president on the mattress up a flight of stairs to a small side room on the depot's second floor. The movement caused Garfield enough pain that he began to faint and then vomit on his outer coat and shirt. Once again, Townshend administered the stimulant. Charles Purvis, one of the few African-American physicians practicing in Washington and surgeon in chief to the Freedmen's Hospital, was the next doctor to turn up. He, too, examined the bullet wound and ordered bottles of hot water placed around Garfield's leg and feet and a blanket wrapped around his torso. This was done to counteract the president's clammy skin, weak pulse, and shallow breathing. To further stimulate his bodily functions, Garfield was told to take a larger swallow of plain brandy. As Townshend and Purvis waited for more senior physicians to arrive, Lincoln and Hunt, not knowing whether the shooting was the act of a lone gunman or some type of coordinated conspiracy, ordered federal troops to maintain positions throughout Washington and to begin closing off the White House.

Lincoln also asked someone to locate Doctor Willard Bliss, telling the physician to come to the railway depot without delay. The fifty-five-year-old Bliss—his given first name was Doctor—was considered an expert in gunshot wounds from his days as a surgeon of the Third Regiment Michigan Infantry during the Civil War and as surgeon in chief to the U.S. Army's Armory Hospital in Washington. (Walt Whitman, in *Specimen Days*, praised Bliss as "one of the best surgeons in the army.") A stout, round-faced man with a

Roman nose, Bliss had slicked-down graying hair, lengthy sideburns, and a chin tuft. He had a forceful personality and was an influential member of the Board of Health of the District of Columbia, having practiced medicine and surgery in the city since the conclusion of the war. Most important, Lincoln knew that Bliss was a boyhood friend of Garfield's and could be trusted to manage the chaotic medical scene at the depot.

In fifteen minutes Bliss arrived and assumed control of all medical decisions. In an effort to determine the direction of the bullet track, he took the little finger of his unwashed and possibly manure-tinged left hand—Bliss had arrived by horse—and, in his words, "passed [it] to its full extent into the wounds."[5] Garfield groaned as Bliss rubbed against a fractured rib and then came into contact with what he believed to be a clot of blood or the surface of the liver. Not satisfied with the digital examination, Bliss took a Nélaton probe, a slender rod of flexible metal with a blunt bulbous tip, and pushed it into the wound's opening hoping to make contact with the bullet. It is very likely that the instrument had not been cleaned from its previous use, and no attempts were made to wash it at the depot. Down it went, almost four inches, until the rounded end became entangled in the bullet-fractured rib fragments. Unable to withdraw the probe, Bliss was forced to press on Garfield's breastbone to relieve the pressure from the splintered rib. When Bliss decided to perform a third investigation, Purvis spoke up and said he objected to any more manipulations. Bliss paid little heed to Purvis and proceeded to take a delicate, curved silver probe and pass it first downward and forward and then downward and backward, "in several directions," according to Bliss's report.[6] From a modern surgical standpoint, it is virtually impossible to determine a bullet's track by either finger or instrument, but Bliss was adamant that the slug had entered Garfield's liver.

By this time, approximately one hour after the shooting, ten physicians were gathered in the room and Bliss was explaining his findings. With Garfield complaining of severe pains in his legs, he asked to be taken to the White House. The team of doctors moved to a corner to decide whether it was safe to accede to Garfield's request. After several minutes of discussion, plans for a speedy removal were agreed upon. Temporary but unclean dressings were applied to the wound. The tension was palpable throughout the panic-stricken station as preparations went forward to move Garfield. "Even before leaving the depot the pressure for admittance to the room where the President was lying was so great that the police could not keep back the crowd," described one eyewitness. "Men persisted that they must see the President, despite the surgeons' orders that the room and hallways must not be filled up."[7] Garfield, still on the mattress, was carried down the winding stairs and through the train station, passing over the floorboards stained with his blood to a waiting horse-drawn police ambulance. Clattering over the forty yards of rough cobblestones of Sixth Street to reach the smooth asphalt pavement of Pennsylvania Avenue, a frightened Garfield, attended by Bliss, Townshend, a third physician, and Rockwell, was jostled to-and-fro, as a surging swarm of thousands struggled to keep up with the charging horses.

Washington became a city in panic. Crowds assembled outside the White House and, once Garfield reached the mansion, the gates of the executive grounds were secured and locked by soldiers and policemen. Nobody was admitted without authority from the president's private secretary. The entire cabinet was told to assemble at the White House and remain there. Blaine sent Vice President Arthur, who was in New York City, a series of telegrams notifying him of the shooting and updating him every few hours on Garfield's condition. But neither Blaine nor any other government official provided instructions regarding what, if anything, Arthur should do in the event of Garfield's incapacity or death. Arthur, who had barely had a civil conversation with Garfield or Blaine since the Robertson nomination was announced in March, sought out his mentor Conkling. They were concerned not only about the threat of additional assassins, but also about the pointed questions being raised regarding Arthur's fitness to assume the presidency. "The effect of [Arthur's] accession to the power and patronage of the Executive office," according to one newspaper account, "was the subject of grave discussions."[8] Most political observers assumed that Conkling would rule if Arthur succeeded Garfield. One reporter noted that Arthur would allow himself to be used "as a cat's-paw by Conkling."[9]

Merchants were anxious, and the bankers, brokers, and speculators on Wall Street were apprehensive about the possible financial repercussions. Most alarming to Arthur and Conkling were the fast-spreading rumors that they and the Stalwarts were in some measure responsible for the tragedy. Veiled threats against their lives were reported, especially when Guiteau's claim to be a Stalwart became widely known. A lengthy editorial in the *New York Times* linked Guiteau's action directly to political factionism within the Republican Party: "[Guiteau's] resentment was inflamed and intensified by the assaults upon the President which have been common in too many circles for the past few months."[10]

Arthur's and Conkling's every movement was chronicled in the dailies. Back and forth they stirred from Arthur's Lexington Avenue residence to Conkling's apartment at the Fifth Avenue Hotel, but no decision was reached about Arthur's return to Washington. At 9:30 P.M., Arthur received a telegram from Hunt and James: "The President is no better, and we fear sinking." Once again, Arthur sought out Conkling's advice, but at that late hour the choice seemed self-evident. Conkling would escort Arthur to Jersey City's train station—reporters even noted that Conkling carried Arthur's baggage—and the vice president would take a midnight train scheduled to arrive in Washington the next morning, Sunday, July 3.

In Elberon, one of Lucretia's aides told her of the shooting. Although little information was available, Garfield's personal assistant wired Lucretia that the president "has been seriously hurt, how seriously he cannot yet say." Minutes later, another telegram arrived from Garfield's private secretary cautioning Lucretia not to believe any "sensational dispatches about the President."[11] By 12:40 P.M., Lucretia, accompanied by friends and associates, was on board a special single Pullman car bound for Washington. At passing stations, she received the latest medical updates concerning her husband's condition. Traveling at over sixty miles per hour, a few minutes south of Baltimore the engine broke down, leaving a frightened and impatient Lucretia stranded. She would not reach the White House until almost 7 P.M.

At police headquarters, a search of Guiteau's clothes found a gun—the arresting officer was so unnerved at the depot that he initially forgot to confiscate the pistol—one letter, and various newspaper articles. "The President's tragic death was a sad necessity, but it will unite the Republican Party and save the Republic," explained Guiteau in the handwritten note. "I had no ill-will toward the President. His death was a political necessity."[12] The newspaper clippings were even more telling. One detailed the resignation of Conkling as senator and others, boldly circled in pencil, concerned the appointment of Robertson. To further emphasize the political nature of his act, Guiteau left, in a thick packet of printed material found at a newsstand in the train depot, a second dispatch. In this one, addressed to General William Tecumseh Sherman, Guiteau referred to himself as a "Stalwart of the Stalwarts," and reminded Sherman that he was a strong backer of Grant.[13] "I am going to jail. Please order out your troops and take possession of the jail at once," he demanded. In addition, Guiteau left behind a memorandum to Arthur informing him of Garfield's assassination and presumptuously outlining his recommendations for a new cabinet.

News that Garfield had been shot shocked the American people. They were soon swept up in the drama as bulletins flashed over newly strung telegraph wires to every frontier town all the way to the Gulf Coast and the Pacific Ocean. Mobs roamed the streets of America's major cities looking for any excuse to riot. Some individuals, when learning of the assassin's foreign-sounding name—Guiteau was born in Illinois of Huguenot background—were convinced that the shooting was a direct result of the country's unchecked immigration policies. Clergymen used their Sunday sermons as opportunities to comment upon the growing lack of religion in American life, pointing out that the tragedy was God's way of calling for greater piety. In New York City, immense crowds gathered in front of the offices of the *New York Herald* where, on a twelve-foot-tall wooden board, the latest medical information was posted. From midsized towns to small villages, citizens sat near the telegraph office waiting for the latest news. Indeed, during these first few days, most individuals were concerned more with Garfield's recovery than with ascribing political or religious blame.

Brought to the second-floor family room at the White House, Garfield continued to complain of severe leg pain. Injections of morphine—hypodermic needles were first widely employed in the United States in the 1870s—were given at 11 A.M. and again at 1 P.M. After the second shot, Garfield suffered an immediate bout of severe nausea and vomiting and said to Bliss, "Well, Doctor, I suppose that was the result of your hypodermic."[14]

Despite this distress, Bliss gave Garfield three more injections of morphine over the course of the afternoon. These shots, and an occasional sip of lime water mixed with milk to control nausea, were the only meaningful medical treatments provided the president during these initial hours. The use of antibiotics, antisepsis, blood transfusions, intravenous fluids, trauma centers, X-rays, let alone simple resuscitative measures, including the monitoring of blood pressure, did not exist. Garfield was lightheaded as his heart beat faster in reaction to his fright and his body's response to the shooting. He breathed rapidly and his forehead was covered with large beads of perspiration. Not wanting to intensify his patient's discomfort or increase the chance of bleeding by unnecessary movements, Bliss ordered that the president remain fully clothed. Finally, at 5:30 in the afternoon, a full eight hours after the shooting, Garfield's shirt and trousers were removed to permit the first thorough physical examination. In view of the state of medicine in 1881, Garfield's recovery—assuming the bullet had not injured any important structures—was going to be based on much good fortune and the problematical process of self-healing.

As Garfield's physiological responses began to slowly compensate for the injury, his condition stabilized. He became relatively upbeat and talkative, and even joked with Bliss about a messenger who was sent for one bottle of brandy but came back with two, and whether he could now have a double dose of stimulant. Garfield asked Blaine the name of the assassin. On being told, he said, "Why should he have wished to shoot me?"[15] Blaine explained that it probably had to do with his disappointment as an office seeker. But Garfield's greatest concern was for the well-being of Lucretia and her return to the White House. He grew impatient waiting for her. When Lucretia arrived, she was ushered upstairs for a private fifteen-minute conversation with her husband. Afterward, she said it was Garfield's courage and calmness that most steadied her and the children.

With twelve doctors congregated in the hallways of the White House, several suggested that despite appearances Garfield was bleeding internally and could not survive the night. Bliss decided that four of them should reexamine the president. One of the physicians, Philip Wales, surgeon general of the U.S. Navy, was asked to digitally explore the bullet track. Garfield's bedclothes and sheets had not been changed for several hours and were saturated, causing him to be uncomfortable from the continuous oozing of blood. Using an unwashed hand, "I inserted my left little finger with a rotary motion," wrote Wales, "and with difficulty, as the aperture of entrance was very small, I distinctly felt the displaced fragments of the broken ribs."[16] Wales concurred with Bliss's assessment that the liver was injured and that Garfield would shortly die. In a last-ditch medical effort, the president was given a glass of champagne that was intended to serve as a tonic to overcome the supposed liver hemorrhage.

Having little else to do, the physicians retired for the night, and Bliss was left to formulate a nursing plan to transform the White House into a hospital. Trained nurses were scarce, so Bliss turned to the wives of various cabinet members to tend to Garfield's needs. The women had no medical knowledge nor did they understand the most basic of nursing responsibilities, but they kept watch and provided a measure of comfort by their presence alone. Garfield slept fitfully, waking up every thirty minutes to vomit. Bliss asked Lucretia's doctor, the homeopathic physician Susan Edson, to supervise the nursing activities.

During these late night hours, Bliss began to issue "official" medical bulletins. Contrasted with ongoing medical realities, the written statements described a far more calm and optimistic situation. "The President has just awakened, greatly refreshed, and has not vomited since 1 A.M.," stated the 4 A.M. report. "The patient is decidedly more cheerful, and has amused himself and watchers by telling a laughable incident of his early career." Two hours later, Garfield was said to have "from the first manifested the most remarkable courage and fortitude." By 11 A.M., the president's condition was described as "greatly improved" and he was "inclined to discuss pleasant topics."[17]

In addition to overseeing the contents of the bulletins—thus controlling what Americans came to know about Garfield's condition and treatment—Bliss began to consolidate his medical authority. Early on Sunday morning, Bliss called together the dozen or so physicians who remained at the White House and told them that the president, the First Lady, and he had evaluated the surgical situation. The doctors' professional services were no longer required. According to Bliss's account, Garfield asked him what his chances of survival were. "Mr. President, your injury is formidable," answered Bliss. "In my judgment, you have a chance for recovery." Garfield grabbed hold of Bliss's arm and said, "Well, Doctor, we'll take that chance."[18] With Bliss's approval, these words were telegraphed all over the country. From then on, secrecy seemed to envelop Garfield's care. With the president's and Lucretia's consent, at least by Bliss's recounting, he was given complete charge of the case with the power to retain and dismiss whomever he chose.

The gathered physicians were astonished at the turn of events. They argued with Bliss about his growing authority. He was accused of egomania and was told that his professional credentials—a private practice, bereft of scholarly achievement—were not worthy of caring for the president. One of the dismissed doctors charged that Bliss had not properly examined Garfield, and it was actually Wales's clinical acumen that led to the discovery of the fractured rib. A flabbergasted Wales alleged that other than for a few "desultory remarks" by Bliss at the gathering of physicians, "it was clearly evident that arrangements had been already made for a change in the consultation."[19] Another physician was quoted in a newspaper saying, "I am afraid Bliss will probe the wound and if he does inflammation will set in and the President will die."[20] Several homeopathic doctors, who had examined Garfield on the day of the shooting, expressed concern that homeopathic principles were not being incorporated into Garfield's daily treatment. They criticized the continuing administration of high doses of morphine, sometimes mixed with large amounts of quinine, as a source of Garfield's intestinal cramping and nausea. Naturally, Bliss disputed all these claims and maintained that his right to manage the case, along with his medical judgments, were based entirely on the Garfields' preference. In Bliss's words, "If I can't save him, no one can."[21]

The medical infighting between Bliss and his Washington-based colleagues worsened. Several hours after the mass firing, Jedediah Baxter arrived at the White House. Baxter, the U.S. Army's chief medical purveyor, who had taken care of Lucretia during her recent bout with malaria, asked Bliss to see the president. Informed that Garfield was not to be disturbed, Baxter responded, "He is my patient. I have prescribed for him for the past five years, and insist on seeing him."[22] Bliss accused Baxter of grandstanding and simply wanting to assume control of the case. Calling Bliss a liar, Baxter lunged toward the door of Garfield's room but Bliss's son pushed Baxter out of the way. Baxter was escorted, by armed guards, from the executive mansion, while the shouting and shoving incident was widely reported in the nation's papers.

The physicians' dismissals, the lack of homeopathic representation, and the Baxter quarrel created considerable debate within the local medical community as pro- and anti-Bliss factions quickly evolved. In the meantime, Garfield, who knew nothing about the doctors' strife, was told to lie still in bed, as Bliss ordered the president not to budge, lest internal bleeding increase. Bliss's concerns were motivated in part by Garfield's fluctuating condition. By late Sunday evening, thirty-six hours after the shooting, Garfield's pulse rate was back up to 120, he was taking twenty breaths per minute, and his temperature was 100 degrees. Looking both to defuse the local squabbling and to spread the medical blame if Garfield should die, Bliss invited David Hayes Agnew, professor of surgery at the University of Pennsylvania School of Medicine in Philadelphia, and Frank Hamilton, professor of surgery at New York City's Bellevue Medical College, to review the management and future treatment of the president.

While Bliss waited for word from Agnew and Hamilton, he asked Joseph Woodward to be his second-in-command, to prepare the daily medical bulletins and to be in charge of taking Garfield's temperature, pulse, and respiratory rate. It was a strange choice. The straitlaced Woodward, who was the newly named president of the American Medical Association, was more a researcher—he was one of the country's earliest experts in the use of a microscope—than a clinician. Indeed, an angry Wales sarcastically noted that "[Dr. Woodward] knew nothing about gunshot wounds, practically, but that he had looked up the matter in the books and found that the way to treat gunshot wounds of the abdomen was the following— reading off the notes."[23] Like many others before him, Woodward stuck his unwashed finger into Garfield's wound only to encounter the same fragments of shattered rib that had ended the other examinations. To complete the team of attending surgeons, Bliss asked Robert Reyburn, professor of anatomy and surgery at Howard University, to maintain daily notes on the case and Joseph Barnes, surgeon general of the U.S. Army, to consult twice a day. Woodward and Reyburn were to sleep each night alternately in the White House and render whatever medical assistance was required.

On the morning of Monday, July 4, Agnew and Hamilton

arrived. The president did not seem worse, although his temperature spiked to 102. When asked by his son how he was doing, Garfield said, "Don't be alarmed, the upper story is all right; it is only the hull that is a little damaged."[24] Bliss briefed the two surgeons on the situation and they then inserted their unwashed instruments into the wound. As Bliss wrote in his official report, "They individually examined the wound with great care. These examinations consisted in the introduction in different directions of probes."[25] With little else to add—Agnew and Hamilton could not determine the course of the bullet but did not believe the liver was injured—a public bulletin was issued stating their satisfaction with all that had been done. Reporters were quick to interview the two surgeons. "When I left Washington at 3 o'clock this afternoon," Hamilton told the New York Times, "President Garfield was no worse than he was at 6:30 o'clock this morning, when I arrived there. There was no evidence that he was sinking—nothing to lead to a suspicion that he was."[26] The president's condition remained stable enough that Bliss did not consider it necessary to have Agnew and Hamilton remain in Washington. They were kept informed by daily telegrams and would not return until July 23.

Medically, Garfield was on his own. There was little that physicians could do. Without the necessary medical and surgical knowledge to more thoroughly understand the president's condition, it was a wait-and-see proposition. Bliss spoke glowingly of Garfield's physical prowess and how this vigor would see him through the crisis. But Garfield would require more than just watchful waiting. His temperature was spiking every evening, sometimes to as high as 103. A surgeon today understands that when a patient has daily temperature increases, this usually indicates the presence of a hidden abscess or a brewing infection. If an abscess is surgically opened, allowing free drainage of its fetid content, then natural immunologic defense mechanisms should overcome the bacteria and the infection will abate. However, if an abscess is left untreated or inadequately incised, it festers and enlarges, and, ultimately, the bacteria metastasize to other locations, leading to irreversible whole body sepsis. Bliss and his team were ignorant of these facts and the relationship between germs, diseases, and death.

In addition to his febrile condition, Garfield had severe gastric distress and could not keep down adequate nourishment. He was slowly wasting away from a spreading infection, unable to be fed and unable to leave his bed. To make matters worse, as Garfield grew sicker, Bliss became more of a medical autocrat and his treatment plans took on an increasingly harsher tone. To isolate Garfield from the outside world (why such total exclusion was medically necessary remains unclear), screens were positioned around the president's bed so that he could no longer look outside. Family and close friends were allowed only limited access. Blaine would not see Garfield again until Thursday, July 21, and then only for a few minutes. Other cabinet officers and high-level government officials were no longer welcomed to the White House. Even Vice President Arthur, who went to the executive mansion to ascertain Garfield's condition on Sunday, July 3, and Tuesday, July 5, was turned away.

Medical and public relations disasters were brewing. The American public closely followed the drama as thrice-daily medical bulletins described a resting and recuperating Garfield, who seemed in no danger of dying: "July 7, 9:15 A.M., the President has passed a most comfortable night, and continues steadily to improve." "July 17, 7 P.M., Our expectations of favorable progress have been fully realized by the manner in which the President has passed the day."[27] The communiqués might have reassured everyone about Garfield's health, but they hid the tribulations of a medical team at odds and flummoxed about how to halt Garfield's slow deterioration. Newspapers were not about to let the story retreat from page one. And, as the medical inconsistencies and bickering slowly came to light, the public began to question the abilities of Bliss and his consultants. Did the physicians know what they were doing or was the true story being hidden? People grew suspicious, and much of the criticism emanated from within the medical profession.

8

The State of
American Medicine

In 1881, American medicine was in the middle of a revolution. Fundamental developments in the medical sciences, including groundbreaking research in bacteriology, histology, pathology, and physiology, heralded a new era in clinical practice. Old-world herbal and mineral concoctions were abandoned in favor of modern pharmaceuticals. Centuries-old therapies, including bleeding, blistering, and purging, fell by the wayside, as physicians began to understand the relationship of bacteria, disease, and the public's health. The most critical qualities of modern medical thought—a scientific attitude, an openness to question past authority, learning from clinical experience, and the need to adapt therapeutic practices accordingly—were becoming mainstays of everyday clinical work. America's healers were emerging from the restraints of ignorance and superstition to become world leaders in medical education and research.

Unfortunately, James Garfield would not benefit at all from this medical revolution. His doctors were mired in medicine of the past and could not conceive of diseases and treatments in anything resembling today's scientific terms. For Bliss and his minions, ancient remedies, old-world philosophies, and a stubborn resistance to scientific progress characterized their every deed and word. In their arrogance and hubris, they would bring about the death of a president of the United States.

At the time of Garfield's shooting, despite remarkable developments in medical thinking, the everyday practice of American medicine remained doctrinally divided. Two of the reasons for the discord—animosities between rival physician factions and a closed-mindedness toward the use of antisepsis—directly affected Garfield's care. Until the 1880s, virtually anyone could call him- or herself a physician and treat patients. Americans embraced this laissez-faire style of health care delivery, and partially as a result of this lack of governmental regulation and control, alternative or sectarian medical groups emerged. They soon successfully lobbied for the repeal of the few state and local licensing laws that were biased toward the dominant medical orthodoxy. In 1847, responding to these challenges, a group of physicians founded an organization to function as a unifying body for traditional-style practitioners. This society, the American Medical Association, provided a sense of socioeconomic stability for its constituents at a time when the day-to-day practice of medicine was in managerial disorder. Despite its supposed mandate, the association held little official authority and, through the time of Garfield's presidency, no federal, state, or local licensing agencies provided well-defined legal standards for medical education, training, and practice.

As a consequence of this turmoil, in the years before and after the Civil War, unregulated orthodox and sectarian medical schools flourished. This medical mishmash meant that an individual could obtain a medical degree and tout himself as either a traditional-style or a sectarian-schooled physician. Even more confusing were the numerous cross-over doctors who switched clinical allegiances in mid-career. To the unschooled layperson, however, legal and scientific distinctions between orthodox doctors and sectarian physicians meant little when choosing a practitioner. In this prescientific era, a healer's clinical identity and reputation were tied more to personal character and bedside manner than to medical know-how.

By 1870, there were two major competing groups of American physicians, allopaths (so-called regular or orthodox) and homeopaths (known as irregular or sectarian), who vied for patient loyalty. Allopaths and homeopaths argued over many aspects of medical care. From drugs and their dosages to physician education and patient evaluations, every clinical subject was open to dispute. "No body of men are less in concert, or seem less influenced by the *espirit du corps*, than physicians," remarked one observer. "The quarrels of physicians are proverbially frequent and bitter, and their hatred, in intensity and duration, seems to exceed that of other men."[1] So acrimonious were these disagreements that allopathic physicians often refused to treat a patient, regardless of how sick the individual was, if a homeopathic doctor was involved in the case.

Allopaths, whose remedies produced effects different from or opposite to those produced by an illness, were in the numerical majority—approximately ten to one—and distinguished themselves by being members of the American Medical Association. These traditional-style physicians are the direct ancestors of today's M.D.'s. They adhered to a brand of therapeutics termed "heroic medicine." Relying on bleeding and blistering, in addition to administering harsh mineral concoctions to induce vomiting and purging, these measures—called "heroic" for their dosage size and effects— were used to treat virtually every known disease and injury. Intended to drive poisonous fluids from the body, such extreme methods were considered state-of-the-art medicine at a time when clinical practice was decidedly nonscientific.

Any healer not embracing "heroic" medicine was deemed an irregular or sectarian practitioner. Regardless of a sectarian's educational background, the one unifying feature of the irregulars was their vocal and emphatic opposition to the allopaths' relentless use of "heroic" therapy. By far, the most widespread and politically powerful of the sectarian movements was homeopathy. Based on a theory antithetical to that of the allopaths, homeopaths promoted a system of therapy that involved minuscule doses of drugs. Since the allopaths' larger doses of drugs were believed to aggravate illness, one of the major principles of homeopathy, the law of infinitesimals, stated that smaller drug dosages are more successful in supporting the vital spirit of the body. Contrary to what allopaths believed, homeopaths accepted as medical gospel the creed that drugs gain potency through massive dilution. Homeopathic enthusiasts were known to carry their convictions to the extreme, believing that dilutions as small as one one-millionth of an allopath's normal dose were effective. Such dilutions were said to be beneficial because the body in illness was more sensitive to drug therapy than it was in health.

Homeopathy was based on experimental pharmacology completed by a German physician, Samuel Hahnemann, during the first half of the nineteenth century. Homeopathy's tenets spread to the United States through the influx of German-speaking immigrants and their doctors, especially in Illinois and Ohio. Though always considered a minority medical philosophy, homeopathy's gentler therapeutics made steady inroads into the nation's health care system. By taking a minimalist approach toward treatment, homeopathic remedies tended not to produce ill effects. This was a welcomed relief from the potent cathartics, emetics, and purgatives, in addition to other bizarre practices, including the outlandish use of scarification and mustard packs to draw toxic fluids and vapors from the body, employed by physicians of the allopathic school. By the 1870s, there were several thousand homeopathic healers, supported by national and state medical societies, dozens of medical colleges, and numerous monthly journals.

As the burgeoning scientific revolution transformed medical behavior, allopathic and homeopathic positions softened and, by the time of Garfield's presidency, their therapeutic philosophies had begun to merge. Younger homeopaths mitigated their dogmatic adherence to Hahnemann's theories, arguing that their sect's key therapeutic principles were scientifically untenable. Many sectarians came to see that their separatist position barred them from important roles in community medical institutions, particularly public hospital staffs and boards of health, thus ensuring their status as second-class medical citizens. Allopaths lessened their resistance to working with homeopaths, having grown disheartened over fruitless fights for therapeutic superiority. Some of the allopaths' acquiescence also stemmed from a realization by the increasing number of allopathic specialists—the beginnings of specialization marked the 1870s and 1880s medical revolution—that homeopathic practitioners could serve as lucrative sources of patient referrals. A new generation of leaders on both sides recognized that nobody was benefiting from the ongoing hostilities. Indeed, as allopaths and homeopaths jointly embraced the rise of modern medical thought, there no longer seemed a need to refer to any physician as a regular or an irregular; they appeared as equals in the court of public opinion.

Rapprochement, however, was not welcomed by all allopaths. Many older physicians, such as Bliss, recalled the acrimony of earlier times and refused to believe that allopaths and homeopaths could ever work together. The allopaths' old guard maintained that if homeopaths wished to practice more allopathic-oriented medicine and maintain staff privileges at allopathic-dominated hospitals and other community institutions, they should no longer call themselves homeopaths. Resistant to change, these unrepentant allopaths continued to foster major rifts within American medicine by refusing to regard homeopathy as a meaningful division within the nation's medical system. Yet to justifiably criticize and ostracize homeopaths, the orthodox profession would have to shed its own reliance on an unscientific past by renouncing many of its therapeutic endeavors, especially the horrible and ineffective "heroic" therapies. Such farsighted thinking—the scientific and professional authority of a kinder and gentler allopathic medicine would not be firmly established in America until the waning years of the nineteenth century—was not part of Bliss's personality. He was a man of firm convictions and indubitable actions. Certainly, the attribution "godlike" accurately described his behavior in the Garfield case.

Arbitrary and imperious, Bliss had little faith in homeopaths' modifying their views or their accepting his.

The Garfields, especially Lucretia, were staunch believers in homeopathic medicine. Several years before, Lucretia had even asked her husband to introduce legislation establishing equal rights in the federal government for homeopathic physicians. When Bliss refused to allow Susan Edson, Silas Boynton, and other homeopaths a say in Garfield's medical decision making, a tempest erupted. "*What a howl* would have gone up from Maine to Texas, and from Cape-Cod to Cape Prince of Wales, had half the blunders already witnessed occurred under homeopathic treatment of the President's case!" wrote one homeopath. "If the treatment of the President be a fair illustration of the *ways, means* and *methods* of so-called *regular* medicine, *Heaven deliver us!*"[2]

The fifty-eight-year-old Edson was the first woman to establish a homeopathic medical practice in Washington. From her clinical experience in Civil War–era hospitals, she was familiar with treating gunshot injuries and their complications, but little of this mattered to Bliss. He regarded Edson as a nurse, and not once during the almost three-month ordeal did Bliss seek her medical advice. Every other night, Edson sat at Garfield's bedside fanning him, rubbing his legs, or encouraging him to take some nourishment. "I felt that I not only cared for him in the ordinary capacity of a nurse," Edson recalled, "but that he gained strength and vitality from me."[3] Though the Garfield children fondly called her "Dr. Edson, full of Med'cin!" and Lucretia regarded Edson as her medical savior, the reticent homeopath rarely voiced public criticism of Bliss's actions.[4]

Boynton did not demonstrate such verbal reserve. A graduate of the same homeopathic medical school as Edson, Boynton was a highly regarded practitioner who lived in Cleveland. A cousin on both sides of the Garfield family, he was frequently summoned to Washington whenever they had a medical crisis. Reduced to the status of a nurse, Boynton chafed under Bliss's professional insult and became the unnamed source of reporters' accounts detailing

Garfield's slow deterioration. Within two weeks of the shooting, newspaper articles described a growing friction between the allopaths and the homeopaths. Arguments were overheard between Bliss and Boynton concerning Boynton's suggestions and services. "It is part of the gossip of the White House," wrote one reporter, "that the attending allopaths have been informed [by Boynton] that Gen. Garfield was not a patient of the state, and that the sickroom would not be made a school for doctors."[5]

Much of the disagreement centered on Garfield's uncontrollable vomiting. Edson and Boynton believed that the "heroic" amounts of morphine and quinine given to Garfield, on a three- or four-times-a-day basis, aggravated his digestion. Both homeopaths knew that Garfield had suffered from stomach problems for years. Yet Bliss and the other allopaths claimed not to be aware of this fact. This suggests that they had never discussed Garfield's medical history with his longtime family physicians. Edson and Boynton were correct in their analysis. Among the common side effects of chronic morphine use are stomach distress, vomiting, and constipation. Garfield suffered from all three. The drugs were causing digestive difficulties and, had Garfield survived, given the dosages of morphine, he might have become addicted.

In addition, Boynton complained to reporters that Garfield was provided too many hard-to-digest foods and alcoholic beverages, none of which calmed his stomach. Furthermore, they lacked nutritional value; homeopaths held that medical treatment must be supported by proper dietetic measures. For example, on July 13, Garfield took four ounces of milk combined with one teaspoonful of rum every two hours during the day. He also chewed the breast of a woodcock for breakfast, but could not swallow the meat. Lunch on July 14 consisted of a sandwich of scraped raw beef, two teaspoonfuls of beef juice, and an ounce of 1868 Tokay wine. Two days later, he had oatmeal and milk, lamb chops, and bacon for breakfast and soon complained of severe abdominal pains. Breakfast on July 18 was steak, poached eggs, potatoes, and toast, all of which he vomited. "As he did not seem to relish solid food," recounted one of Garfield's doctors, "it was deemed best to give him chiefly liquids and in diminished quantities."[6] Garfield was rapidly losing weight and, without adequate nourishment, he stood little chance of healing.

Throughout the remainder of the summer, reporters hunted down rumors of frequent clashes between Boynton and Bliss. "We were placed in a trying and perhaps peculiar position, for the reason that we are both homeopathists," recounted Edson. "It was especially hard for Dr. Boynton to be placed in the position he held, as one of the nurses, inasmuch as he was an intimate personal friend of the patient's."[7] Bliss denied everything while Boynton continued to stoke the gossip mill. In mid-August, an exasperated Boynton confronted the Garfields and asked how Bliss came to be the president's physician. Although the answer was initially kept private, within a month of Garfield's death, Boynton issued a public communiqué about the medical care. In a two-page handwritten letter, Boynton noted that Garfield had told him that he actually considered Jedediah Baxter to be his physician and that neither the president nor his wife had ever asked Bliss to take charge. Boynton's declaration could be dismissed as mere resentment toward Bliss, except that the dispatch also contained an attached handwritten note from Lucretia: "I have read the statement of Doctor Boynton made this day and will say that it is entirely correct."[8]

Boynton's criticism concerning the inappropriateness of "heroic" therapy and Garfield's lack of nutrition was accurate. However, whether a decrease in the morphine and quinine alone could have saved Garfield's life is doubtful. Certainly, the president would have been more comfortable and without the feeling of constant nausea. But changing neither drugs nor diet would negate the outdated and unsafe manner in which the bullet wound was managed. Many homeopaths and allopaths agreed that the proper use of Joseph Lister's recently introduced system of antisepsis might have changed the ultimate outcome. "I think the President had a reasonable chance for recovery, but it was thrown away by the bad man-

agement of the case," Boynton told a reporter. "During the first
three weeks when everything depended upon the utmost skill, it
was then that the wound was not properly cleansed."⁹ How was
it that Bliss and the other physicians, all highly educated and immensely influential, were so lacking in their clinical judgments,
especially concerning antisepsis and the bullet wound? Why did
they have such little faith in Lister's research? As Harriet Blaine, the
wife of the secretary of state, wrote, "It has always seemed to me
that the surgeon's skill ought to have saved Garfield. Perhaps had it
been wisely exerted, it would."¹⁰

There were few more fundamental discoveries in medicine than
Lister's brilliant insight in the mid-1860s that to destroy germs on a
wound or to prevent their entrance into the injury will lessen the
chance of an infection. Lister soaked his surgical sponges and bandages in a carefully prepared antiseptic solution of carbolic acid and
even used an atomizer to spray the liquid over the wound during an
operation. More important, he stressed that his antiseptic system
must also include instrument washing, hand rinsing, and wound
cleaning if bacterial contamination was to be lessened. Yet in July
1881, many American physicians were not ready to embrace Lister's breakthrough concept. Stories abounded about surgeons,
allopaths, and homeopaths alike, who halfheartedly embraced Listerism by working with what they considered clean operative sites,
but then sneezed into their hands and proceeded to manipulate
wounds. "We operated in old blood-stained and often pus-stained
coats," reminisced one surgeon. "We operated with clean hands in
the social sense, but they were undisinfected hands." Acknowledg-
ing his ignorance of germs, he recalled, "If there was any difficulty in
threading the needle we moistened it with saliva, and rolled it
between bacteria-infected fingers."¹¹

Many doctors claimed to be Lister acolytes, but it was difficult to
distinguish between strict adherence to Lister's antisepsis in practice and use of his antiseptic system in name only. The simple fact
was that medicine could not truly evolve until the grave problem of

controlling infection was resolved. Infectious diseases, especially blood poisoning, were of paramount concern for any patient, particularly those with gunshot injuries. However, without an understanding and acceptance of the existence of bacteria, most physicians could do little more than provide generally ineffective attempts at surgical cleanliness and gentle wound manipulation.

Lister, an Englishman, was changing the face of European medicine, but wide acceptance of his antiseptic system in America, much to the discredit of the country's physicians, was several years away. For now, there was a generational divide. Younger men generally supported Lister's ideas and older men pooh-poohed them. "But these [details], one should remember, are the words of a theorist," an older doctor wrote of Lister's findings, "who, as the Italians wittily say of such, has a grasshopper in his head."[12] Bliss was never a true believer in Lister's work or the linking of germs to pus and disease, although he pointed out that "most approved antiseptic dressings were used during the entire progress of the case."[13] He said this despite having allowed over a dozen physicians, including himself, to probe Garfield's bullet wound with unwashed instruments and dirt-encrusted and, probably at times, horse manure–laden fingers. The younger generation of American doctors asked that Bliss and his team pay more attention to the details of Lister's antiseptic system, but these youthful physicians were neither the decision makers nor the influential voices within the profession.

It was not as if Bliss and his associates were unfamiliar with Lister's work—they simply had little confidence in its soundness. The basis for this lack of faith can be traced to a lecture Lister had given five years earlier, at the International Medical Congress held in Philadelphia as part of the 1876 Centennial Anniversary of the Declaration of Independence. The congress was a sizable gathering attended by almost five hundred doctors, and Lister was the most eminent foreigner present. A slender man, five feet ten inches in height, with ruddy cheeks and flyaway muttonchops, the fifty-year-old surgeon was honored by being asked to serve as president of the congress's Surgical Section. Lister told his hosts—who included

Agnew, Hamilton, and Woodward—that "American surgeons are renowned throughout the world for their inventive genius, and boldness and skill in execution." He reminded them that it was to America that the world owed anesthesia, "the greatest boon ever conferred upon suffering humanity by human means." And he informed them that he was there to perform important missionary work, specifically for the principles of antisepsis, because American surgeons, unlike many of their European colleagues, had been slow to embrace his concepts. "I should be pleased, indeed, if the discussion which is about to take place should have the effect of strengthening the belief of the profession in the truth, the value, and the practical application of the principles of Antiseptic Surgery."[14]

Lister gave a three-hour discourse explaining the details of his antiseptic system, concentrating on the relationship of bacteria, pus, and wound infection. As strange as it sounds today, physicians in the pre-Listerian era regarded the presence of pus as a positive sign of wound healing. Traumatic wounds, especially gunshot injuries, were thought to be lined with dead tissue that was expelled in the form of purulent matter. When a wound healed without an abundant flow of what was politely termed "laudable pus," it was considered an aberration. Lister would change this millennia-old belief and teach physicians that a healthy wound contains no pus. He explained to the American audience that among the major tenets of antisepsis was preventing access to infecting organisms at the site of potential infection. Bullet wounds should never be manipulated with unclean instruments and unwashed fingers must never enter a bullet's track. Lister even gave a practical demonstration of the antiseptic system on an actual patient.

"Modesty is stamped upon his every act and word," wrote one eyewitness, "and he *does* believe in antiseptic surgery."[15] But, in Philadelphia, Lister's doubters dotted the audience. Hamilton contested the English surgeon's claims. "A large proportion of American surgeons seem not to have adopted the practice," said Hamilton, "whether from a lack of confidence or for other reasons I cannot say." Hamilton pointed out that some physicians had developed competing methods for treating wounds "for which their advocates claim exceptional and extraordinary results."[16] The president of the overall congress, a doyen of American surgery, had the last word when he stated, "Little, if any faith, is placed by any enlightened or experienced surgeon on this side of the Atlantic in the so-called [antiseptic] treatment of Professor Lister."[17]

Not easily dissuaded, Lister and his wife set out on an evangelistic transcontinental train journey. He was going both to explore America and to proselytize to its surgeons. In September 1876, the American Wild West still existed—three months earlier the Sioux, under chief Crazy Horse, had annihilated Colonel George Custer and his band of soldiers at the Little Big Horn—but the Listers dutifully traveled over the Rockies to San Francisco and back via Salt Lake City and Chicago. In the Windy City, Lister impressed local doctors when they met one of his former patients from Glasgow, a recent émigré to the United States, who had been cured by Lister's antiseptic methods of wound dressing during the late 1860s. Leaving the Midwest, Lister headed to Boston, where he knew several prominent Harvard surgeons. Among them, thirty-four-year-old John Collins Warren was his most vigorous advocate. Warren had studied with Lister in Glasgow in 1869 and, later that year at Massachusetts General Hospital, performed a mastectomy using Listerian antisepsis. Warren's enthusiasm for antiseptic surgery, however, was tempered by more senior Harvard physicians who were less enamored of Lister's technique and decided against its widespread use in the hospital.

Lister and his wife returned to New York City early in October. Speaking at Charity Hospital, he honored a request to perform a surgical operation before a crowded audience of medical students and surgeons. He merely opened a groin abscess to drain a pocket of pus, but it was a useful and practical demonstration. Lister stressed the need for cleanliness, especially the requirement to bathe one's hands in an antiseptic solution prior to touching a patient (rubber surgical gloves had not yet been invented) or manipulating a wound. "His minute attention to all such details made this lecture of unusual interest and importance," noted an eyewitness.[18] Two days later, the Listers sailed for London, uncertain of Joseph's success in convincing American doctors of the importance of antisepsis.

Lister had good reason to doubt whether his talks succeeded. It had been a decade and a half since he had first introduced the concept of antisepsis, but of all the countries he lectured in, American doctors seemed the least impressed. It was not that Americans were unfamiliar with Lister's findings. Young doctors from North America, who were completing their medical education in Europe, had visited and worked with him in Glasgow and Edinburgh. These twenty- and thirty-year-olds returned to America imbued with an enthusiasm for the antiseptic method. They experimented with antisepsis, wrote articles describing their medical successes, and attempted to interest their colleagues. The older doctors listened politely, but few were ready to accept the new teachings, especially the underlying notion that related microscopic organisms, so-called germs, to pus, infection, and disease.

There were other explanations as to why America's doctors seemed reluctant to embrace Listerism. Lister's system of hand washing, instrument cleaning, and spraying the skin with an antiseptic solution proved burdensome. Even when surgeons supposedly abided by Lister's rules, there were notable failures. But there was another overriding reason why Americans delayed adopting antisepsis. A physician's choice of clinical treatment was best determined by his educational background and, in nineteenth-century America, there was a vast indifference in medical schools to the basic medical sciences. Although it now seems axiomatic that the clinical practice of medicine derives daily sustenance from scientific research, such was not the case in American medicine during the eighteenth and much of the nineteenth centuries. It was still a time of newly established political independence, with each physician and medical school proclaiming its own brand of medical independence. The unscientific basis of medical practice—the physician's drugs and other remedial substances were unchanged from those utilized since the time of Hippocrates—the hodgepodge of therapeutic philosophies, and the haphazard system of medical education and training made it impossible to prove or disprove the soundness of most medical claims or the competency of any doctor.

Among the reasons why these difficulties existed was the very nature of the country itself. The combination of hard-won political freedoms, the remnants of Jacksonian-style individualism, and the economic opportunities available on the resource-rich land led to a neglect of the less practical or theoretical sciences, particularly those relevant to medicine. In the settling of such a massive and rugged place, practical-minded Americans sought the simplest means to exploit the environment and foster their own comfort and safety. As a result, innovative and intellectual pursuits in the medical sciences, at least until the 1870s, were thwarted by the nation's socioeconomic and political conditions.

With almost no basic scientific research being conducted until a decade after the Civil War, medical education was focused chiefly on getting the patient well, to the exclusion of everything else, especially the medical sciences. Consequently, older physicians, such as Bliss, Agnew, Hamilton, and Woodward, had little understanding of the new sciences of bacteriology and pathology. With such poor background in the basic sciences, the older doctors could appreciate neither the fundamentals of Lister's theories nor the practical implications of his work. It was incomprehensible to them that recently discovered microbes could be the cause of so many problems. Finally, there were those American physicians who agreed about the importance of antisepsis, but not as it applied to them. Since these doctors worked in the American countryside, where the air was considered nothing less than pure, they felt they need not worry about bacteria or the application of Listerian principles.

From the moment that Bliss first placed his finger and instruments into Garfield's wound, the president's health was compromised. What had been a relatively clean bullet track was transformed into a highly contaminated one. Most wound infections do not become clinically evident for three to five days. It takes that amount of time for the bacterial inoculum to increase in size and produce symptoms, in particular fever spikes. Such was not the case with Garfield, whose temperature, within forty-eight hours, was up to 102. Scientifically unaware of Garfield's medical predicament—a wound infection was never considered as a possible cause of fever—Bliss confidently predicted full recovery, but the relapsing nature of the president's condition required an explanation.

Initially, malaria, long endemic in Washington, with its accompanying paroxysms of chills and muscle aches, was blamed for Garfield's fever. The White House was situated near large swamps and the supposed perils of bad air and odoriferous gases, given off by rotting plants—so-called miasmas—were well documented. The fear of malaria, also known as marsh miasma, was the reason why Bliss prescribed massive amounts of quinine for Garfield. When this treatment failed to quell the president's temperature problems, the city's oppressive summer heat—usually over 85 degrees during the day—was held accountable. The president grew so uncomfortable from the humidity that blocks of ice were placed in his room. Because the ice did not suffice, a rudimentary air-conditioning unit, the nation's first, was built in the White House. It was a Rube Goldberg–like contraption, consisting of a series of Turkish towels placed inside a massive cast-iron chamber. The towels were kept wet by a solution of ice, water, and salt sprayed on them from above. Fans circulated air through the cloths and the cold exhaust was directed into Garfield's room. This proved inadequate and United States Navy engineers jury-rigged even larger fans and a second cooling unit. Supplying twenty-three thousand cubic feet of air per hour, at a temperature of 54 degrees, the bedside temperature was maintained steadily at 75 degrees day and night.

When the cooling apparatus did not alleviate Garfield's temperature spikes—nothing available in 1881 could possibly have reversed the untreated multiplication of the microbes—Bliss provided other

clarifications. "The real cause of the relapse," according to one contemporary account, "was due to too much exertion, too much food,
and the manipulations of a colored barber."[19] Apparently a barber
was summoned without Bliss's approval to trim the president's
beard, hair, and mustache. The barber asked Garfield to sit up but,
when Bliss walked in unannounced, the doctor grew livid at his patient's supposed barber-induced weariness. Later, when Garfield's
temperature had its usual nighttime increase, Bliss pointed to the
tonsorial session as that day's reason for the president's difficulties.

One week after the shooting, Garfield's wound began to dis-
charge what his doctors referred to as "healthy looking pus."[20] The
president grew restless as his heart and breathing rate ran up, all
consistent with a growing infection. "We do not regard this as unfavorable under the circumstances," Bliss assured a worried public.[21]
Indeed, the team of physicians was so sanguine about the situation
that they confidently predicted the flow of pus might continue for
just a day or two. The doctors were wrong in their assessment. The
outpouring of the putrid mix only intensified and served as a daily
barometer of Garfield's worsening state.

From this time on, Garfield's course became a series of inter-
rupted clinical crises and recoveries, marked by a slow and
inevitable deterioration. Forbidden by Bliss to engage in extended
conversation—a method of conserving strength—Garfield began to
compose sentences into a single expression. When one of his attendants told him that the "heart of the people was in bed with him,"
the president replied, "Sore heart."[22] In mid-July, in a more telling
occurrence, Garfield asked for some writing materials. Lying on his
back, he scribbled his name and the prophetic phrase, "Strangulatus
pro Republica" (strangled for the Republic).[23] Initially, Garfield
showed an outward cheerfulness, but as his recovery dragged on a
sense of the inevitable colored his attitude. "I wonder if all this fight
against death," he remarked to Lucretia, "is worth the little pinch of
life I will get anyway?"[24]

Repeatedly, Bliss reported that Garfield's wound was being
treated in an antiseptic manner. To Garfield's doctors, this meant that

the orifice of the bullet's entry site was swabbed with an antibacterial solution—either carbolic acid, phenol, or potassium permanganate—after which the fluid was injected into the opening to bathe the underlying tissue. However, the physicians continued to probe Garfield's wound with dirty instruments and placed unwashed rubber tubes inside the bullet's track to facilitate drainage of pus. "Here again was the fatal mistake," wrote one reporter. "Day after day the burrowing pus was aided on its way downward among the tissues by the disturbing tubes of the surgeons."[25] Pockets of pus formed under the skin of Garfield's back, but Bliss did not believe that this expanding collection of "laudable" pus could slow the president's recovery.

On Friday, July 22, Garfield's wound discharged a large quantity of purulent material, including a "morsel of sloughing fibrous tissue and a number of adhering fibers of cotton and wool."[26] Woodward examined the one-quarter-inch-square specimen under a microscope. He confirmed it was a portion of the president's cotton shirt, with a few fibers of wool from the coat. In doing this, Woodward conducted the first microscopic-based forensic science examination in the United States. Despite the doctors' jubilation over the sizable amount of drained pus, Garfield had taken a visible turn for the worse. He began to suffer "rigors," an antiquated term for shaking chills accompanied by a high fever (104 degrees) and a rapid heart rate (120 beats per minute).

Rigor was a warning that portended "blood poisoning," a phrase with which physicians in 1881 were well acquainted. Garfield was drenched in sweat, his skin was cool to the touch, and he had an anxious look on his face, all signs of widespread septicemia or pyemia. Though he was restless, the president complained of overwhelming fatigue. His mind wandered and delirium set in. As Bliss eyed the ever-enlarging pus pocket on Garfield's back, a feeling of dread emerged. On Saturday, July 23, Boynton informed reporters that the president was dying: "Pus had through carelessness and neglect been allowed to be in the wound till it rotted and pyemia had done its perfect work."[27] The afternoon papers were filled with stories of Garfield's impending death. Crowds filled the streets waiting for the next bit of news. Bliss and his associates had little else to medically offer the president. Having run out of clinical options, the doctors sought outside assistance. "On account of the unfavorable change that has taken place," Bliss told the assembled journalists, "it was deemed best to telegraph for the consulting surgeons."[28] Agnew and Hamilton were summoned and everyone in the White House, from the physicians to the kitchen staff to Garfield's personal attendants, waited to hear what to do next.

9

Eighty Days

In a medical case of inexplicables, the appearance of David Hayes Agnew and Frank Hamilton provided another baffling incident. The two surgeons arrived at the White House shortly after eight o'clock on Saturday night, July 23. Despite Garfield's worsening condition, Bliss decided it was best not to disturb him. The president was in the middle of another rigor, his fifth in less than twenty-four hours. As the microbes multiplied and the abscesses enlarged, Agnew and Hamilton went to sleep. Garfield would be available for examination the following day. On Sunday morning, with their patient drenched in sweat and struggling for his life, Bliss and his surgical consultants agreed that the wound was not draining adequate amounts of pus—a second opening was needed.

Without anesthesia, without antisepsis, but with dirty fingers and unwashed instruments, Agnew, assisted by Hamilton, made a surgical incision two inches in length and an inch and a half in depth, reaching into the lower levels of the pus pocket. It was an exercise in surgical incompetence. The two surgeons, considered to be among America's best, misjudged the clinical situation. Their incision was not long enough, and two days later, again without antisepsis or anesthesia, the opening needed to be enlarged. Fragments of rib were removed and two bacteria-laden drainage tubes were fastened in place. "During the operation the President displayed his usual courage," noted one reporter. "He neither flinched nor moved."[1] If there was any veracity to these claims, it was because Garfield was confused and dazed from a spreading infection and not a demonstration of manliness. Adding to Garfield's misery, just hours after the second operation, Bliss invited Alexander Graham Bell, the inventor of the telephone, to demonstrate a newfangled electromagnetic bullet-finding device he had recently invented.

From the first minutes following the assassination, finding the bullet had been the primary goal. The physicians thought that if it could be located and removed, then Garfield's life might be spared. For weeks, Bliss and his colleagues had poked and probed the wound—X-rays were not discovered until the mid-1890s—in an attempt to determine the slug's track. They concluded that the projectile had entered the president's back and struck a rib. This caused the bullet to deflect downward, pass through the liver, and come to rest in the muscles of the right mid-abdominal wall. Many doctors disagreed with Bliss's assessment and, in this era of medical individuality, these men were more than willing to air their views.

Within days of the shooting, one exuberant New York surgeon fired shots into several cadavers hoping to replicate Garfield's injury. He concluded that Bliss was only half right. The projectile was on Garfield's right side, but deeper than originally thought. When Bliss, Agnew, and Hamilton noted a hard lump near Garfield's right groin—the swelling would later turn out be another collection of pus—the New Yorker's beliefs became not only acceptable but somewhat corroborative of Bliss's judgment. Bliss and his consultants made certain the findings were widely reported to journalists. Other professionals, however, were dismissive of the results. "The experiments are of little value," wrote one doubter. "I would suggest that the surgeon make the experiment on the assassin, provided he is a skilled marksman."[2]

There was also the theory of a recent medical school graduate, who entirely disagreed with Bliss. Basing his anatomical conclusions on information obtained from newspapers, this medical novice drew diagrams showing the bullet traveling downward and sideways, passing through the president's vertebral bones, and lodging in the left side of Garfield's back, the exact opposite of Bliss's thinking. The doctor even had the temerity to show his drawings to two of the physicians who had examined Garfield at the train station. These men were among the group of doctors later dismissed by Bliss, however, and the young physician's information never made it to the White House. The neophyte, in awe of the president's doctors' reputations, let the matter rest. "I felt that it was improper to urge views which were diametrically opposed to those of gentlemen of acknowledged skill and experience who had had an opportunity of examining the wound."[3] The sad irony was that the young doctor was correct in his clinical hypothesis.

As physicians debated the bullet's whereabouts, suggestions for help flooded into the White House. Boxes filled with letters came daily, from bankers to blacksmiths to housewives, all wanting to assist the medical staff with various treatment plans. One man recommended hanging the president upside down by his toes and allowing the bullet to fall out. Another urged that a rubber tube connected to an air pump be pushed deep into the wound and suction applied to extract the ball. In a more serious suggestion, a country doctor from Kansas telegraphed Lucretia: "Do not allow probing the wound," he pleaded. "Saturate everything with [Lister's] carbolic acid, one part to 20 parts water about. Use quite freely of this about the wound. Probing generally does more harm than the ball."[4] The question of where the bullet had gone took on a preposterous tone when the Washington *Evening Star* published a letter in which a mentally deranged Marylander claimed that the slug had mysteriously appeared in his house. But the suggestions, none of which were heeded, were all for naught.

It was never evident what Bliss was going to do if the bullet was found. Indeed, in the post–Civil War era, it was the norm for a gunshot victim to walk around with pieces of lead inside him. The constant prodding and searching of Garfield served little purpose. Bliss and his consultants could accomplish nothing—the damage from the infection was far more extensive than they realized—even if they knew where the slug resided. However, Bliss's investigations into the bullet's location had consumed so much time—all to Garfield's detriment—and were so widely publicized, that it did not seem unreasonable for a citizen as illustrious as Alexander Graham Bell to be invited to join the hunt. Bell's development of the telephone in 1876 had led to several alternative applications of the new technology to the field of medicine. For example, he conceived of an audiometer for the testing of hearing. Bell also realized that the induction balance, part of a telephone's internal workings, might be used to detect metal within the body. The essential principle was that a metallic object, when placed into the electromagnetic field of a balanced, induced current, would upset the machine's equilibrium and a sound would be heard on the telephone.

Shortly after the assassination attempt, Bell offered his services to Bliss. On Tuesday, July 26, the inventor was ushered into Garfield's room, where Bell was shocked by the president's appearance: "His face is very pale, or rather it is of an ashen grey color which makes one feel for a moment that you are not looking upon a living man."[5] Garfield was turned on his side and Bell placed the device near where he was told the bullet should be. A calibrated balance was not obtained—the device was configured improperly—and the hoped-for clicking noise was not heard. A discouraged Bell spent several days fixing the problem and returned to the White House on the morning of Monday, August 1. The results were equivocal at best, but Bell, looking to protect his reputation as one of the nation's leading scientific men, wrote an official report verifying the location of the bullet ("in a space about two inches in diameter, somewhat to the right, and four and a half inches below the umbilicus") while extolling the virtues of his machine.[6] "The instrument was tested for sensitiveness several times during the course of the experiments," Bell informed Bliss, "and it was found to respond well to the presentation of a flattened bullet at a distance of about four inches from the coils."[7] Naturally, Bliss released the findings to a waiting public as newspapers proclaimed the test a wonderful success.

In actuality, Bell's attempt to locate the bullet proved unsuccessful. The false-positive reading, however, supported Bliss's contention that the bullet was where he said it was, in Garfield's abdominal wall. Although he never stated it directly in his report, Bell seemed to indicate that he tested only the right side of the president's body, since exploration of the left side would have indicated doubt about Bliss's diagnostic abilities. In his later presentations, Bell backtracked from his findings, explaining that metal mattress springs—supposedly he had been assured by Bliss that all metal had been removed from the area of Garfield's bed—caused interference and, as the autopsy was to show, "the bullet was at too great a distance from the surface to have affected our apparatus."[8] As time passed, Bell became even more concerned that his collaboration with Bliss had tainted his scientific reputation. "I feel all the more mortified because I feel that I have really accomplished a great work," he confided to his wife, "and have devised an apparatus that will be of inestimable use in surgery, but this mistake will react against its introduction."[9]

Over the next six weeks, Garfield endured numerous surgical drainages of abscesses; one was so extensive that it necessitated general anesthesia. "The effects of the etherization," according to an eyewitness, "were somewhat distressing, and the shock of the operation no doubt told unfavorably on the President's small reserve of vitality."[10] Improvement in the president's condition never followed, and pus pockets materialized throughout his body. Each time, Bliss insisted that the latest operation would prevent the further spread of blood poisoning, and, in every instance, he was incorrect. In late August, a virulent carbuncle developed in Garfield's right parotid gland—saliva-producing tissue located in front of the ear—causing excruciating pain, swelling of his eye and cheek, and paralysis of his face. His doctors thought that the parotid inflammation was caused by a metastatic infection. They were probably wrong. Parotiditis, with abscess formation and rapidly spreading cellulitis, is common in debilitated and dehydrated patients, the result of thickened saliva that blocks the gland's ducts. Repeated lancings failed to cure the problem. Several days later, the pus spontaneously evacuated through both Garfield's right ear canal and the inside of his mouth. The flood of viscous saliva mixed with pus became so great that he was in danger of drowning in his own spittle. As the infection spread through his head, the jaw muscles became fixed and precluded Garfield from opening his mouth. The beginnings of pneumonia were detected. So deadly was the president's mix of bacteria that, while incising one of his many abscesses, Bliss cut his own finger and developed an infection. Unlike the unlucky president, Bliss's injury healed itself.

On the morning of Sunday, August 14, day forty-four of the ordeal, Garfield vomited what little breakfast he had eaten and continued to retch throughout the afternoon and evening. All food by mouth was stopped and feedings by rectum were begun and would continue until the president's death. Nutritive enemas—consisting of beef bouillon, egg yolks, milk, whiskey, and several drops of opium to decrease colonic irritability—were given. Garfield's flatulence became intolerable and the enema formula had to be tinkered with on a daily basis. Bliss and his medical counselors extolled their decision to institute rectal feeding: "There is every reason to believe that this saved the President from rapidly impending death."[11] The assertion was little more than self-congratulatory rhetoric. Modern medicine has shown that no individual can receive long-term sustenance strictly through rectal feedings.

Garfield was literally starving to death. His ribs protruded, both legs looked like matchsticks, and, as the abscesses grew, he was rotting from the inside out. He could not sit upright, and bed sores and pustules formed over his body. His attendants repositioned him almost one hundred times a day attempting to resolve the problem, but with little success. In less than two months, Garfield's weight had plummeted from a robust 225 pounds to an emaciated 130 pounds. At their wits' end, the doctors came up with various harebrained schemes to improve Garfield's well-being. The U.S. Navy steamer *Tallapoosa* was outfitted at great expense to take Garfield on cruises up and down the Potomac River to provide fresh air. A suite of four rooms, including an onboard bathroom and swinging bed, was readied. But the president, so weakened by his medical care, never set foot on the boat. One morning, Bliss insisted that his room be thoroughly aired and the carpets and upholstered furniture carted away. The president was placed in an adjacent room and commented on how much he enjoyed the change of scenery. There was even talk of redoing the plumbing throughout the executive mansion, as a way to reduce offensive smells thought to cause disease.

On Friday, July 29, Garfield presided over a brief cabinet meeting. The gathering was called to provide Garfield with the impression that he could still complete his duties. The meeting was a sham, however, scheduled strictly for appearance's sake, with the department heads instructed by Bliss not to upset the president with any real difficulties. Within days, Garfield's mental competency became intermittently questionable and remained that way until his death. Because he and Vice President Arthur were political rivals and disliked each other, Garfield's advisers and his physicians never allowed Arthur to see the president or assume any presidential duties. Earlier, Roscoe Conkling had tried to intervene by calling at the White House and asking that his card be given to Lucretia. He was not invited in, and that summer the New York State legislature had ended Conkling's political career by failing to reelect him to the United States Senate. "I am glad it is over," remarked a weary Garfield. "He made a great mistake in my judgment."[12]

The only bona fide executive business that Garfield completed during his illness was the signing of an extradition treaty to return a jailed forger to Canada. On that same day, he also handwrote a letter to his mother telling her not to worry about his condition: "It is true I am still weak, and on my back; but I am gaining every day, and need only time and patience to bring me through."[13] Facsimile copies of the note were spread all over the country as a demonstration of the president's unshaken resolve. Still, even in his lucid moments, Garfield existed in a world of strict isolation from outside events. One of Garfield's attendants could not "remember that he ever but once attempted to smile."[14] Visitors were shooed away and the president's children were no longer permitted to see him. In fact, from the third day after the shooting until Garfield's passing, Bliss kept such tight control over the comings and goings of those who entered Garfield's room that not more than a dozen persons, excluding the physicians, were allowed access. Reporters told of an awkwardness when they stood in the president's private secretary's room, only a few feet away from the sickroom, knowing that so few individuals had actually seen Garfield. In effect, for most of the summer of 1881, the United States of America was without a functioning chief executive.

Through it all, Bliss and his team appeared unaware of the private and public commotion over the president's condition. "Doctor, you seem to be feeling pretty well this morning," a newspaper correspondent commented to Bliss in late summer. "I should think I was," responded the president's chief physician. "Why, the man is convalescent; his pulse is now down to ninety-six."[15] The pronouncement was astounding and the journalist, knowing Garfield's true condition, silently wondered whether Bliss was delirious himself. From the outset, Bliss intended the public bulletins to be deceptive. Caring for a patient who was fully observant and wanting to know everything—Garfield insisted that newspapers be read to him—Bliss chose to withhold negative news about the president's condition from reporters. "These bulletins were often the subject of animated and sometimes heated discussion between Dr. Bliss and the other attending surgeons," according to one eyewitness, "the surgeons usually taking one side of the question and Dr. Bliss the other."[16] Bliss always prevailed, telling his critics that he did not want to dishearten Garfield by circulating discouraging reports. Even as Garfield's mental capacity declined and the reading of newspapers was no longer part of his daily routine, Bliss remained committed to a course of public fraud.

Both the profession and the public grew incensed by Garfield's case. "The Profession cannot fail to regret the character of the bulletins issued," intoned one physician. "They are not only incorrect in regard to the pathology of the case, but they are professionally vague and ambiguous; and worse than all, the diction is so bad that a schoolboy would with ease indicate the grammatical errors so often manifested."[17] A lead editorial in the New York Daily Tribune lambasted Bliss: "It is the duty of a physician to care for his own reputation at the same time that he guards the life of his patient, and, at this stage of the case, with the whole country aware of the gravity of the crisis, no physician, even if he knew no higher moral law than a selfish desire to protect his professional fame, should hold out hope when he knows the event will prove him a false prophet."[18]

As relations between Garfield's doctors and the press deteriorated, the physicians refused to admit anything was untoward. Some newspapers ceased carrying the daily medical bulletins, believing they misled the public. Other sources of information were sought. Silas Boynton and Susan Edson were more than eager to tell journalists that they had abandoned all hope. David Hayes Agnew and Frank Hamilton discussed the situation quite freely, expressing the opinion that Garfield was on the mend. "I have no doubt whatever of his ultimate recovery," Hamilton told one reporter.[19] Conflicting viewpoints abounded, and few individuals seemed certain as to what was truly occurring. The country's doctors argued among themselves while the lay public was lost in an avalanche of medical terms. Did Garfield have pyemia, septicemia, or was it blood poisoning? Most important, would the president survive?

As August turned into September, Garfield's frustrations with his slow convalescence grew evident. He asked to leave Washington, but his physicians and political advisers cautioned against it. On the morning of Monday, September 5, a petulant Garfield decided that he was tired of Bliss's excuses. "Well, is this the last day in the White House?" demanded the president. Bliss tried to quiet his patient, but Garfield insisted, "No, no, I don't want any more delay."[20] Once Garfield's pleading turned into an abrupt command, the doctors and Lucretia quickly decided to move him to the healthy sea air of Elberon—where Lucretia had recently recuperated from malaria—to a house lent by a political admirer.

The Garfields, their physicians, and the president's retinue of attendants would leave Washington the following morning by train. It was the sixty-sixth day of Garfield's ordeal. Hamilton was sent ahead to Elberon to make certain that medical arrangements were in place, including the stocking of emergency first-aid stations along the route should Garfield turn acutely ill. On the New Jersey shore, facing summer air as hot as a blast furnace, several hundred engineers and workmen gathered ties and rails and feverishly laid 3,200 feet of temporary railroad track from the town's small train station to the door of Garfield's seaside cottage-to-be. Assisted by their wives, who provided refreshments, the men labored through the night under the illumination of thousands of lanterns. By 6 A.M. on September 6, the work was finished and, as news spread that Garfield was coming, thousands of the curious descended on the seaside resort.

In a well-planned Washington farewell, also occurring at 6 A.M., a weakened Garfield, struggling to lift his hand, waved good-bye to the White House staff. It was the first time many of them had seen him since the shooting. He was carried on a stretcher to a horse-drawn wagon and taken to a waiting train. "In his general contour, there was something to suggest the face of Garfield to those who had known him long and intimately," noted one eyewitness, "but the change was astounding to everyone unaccustomed to the daily observations of his progress. Perhaps it was not the face of a dying man, but many observers thought it was."[21]

Officials of the Pennsylvania Railroad furnished a four-car train and outfitted one of the cars with an extra-thick mattress on springs intended to decrease the train's rocking motion. Wire gauze was fastened on the outside of the windows to prevent dust from entering. Ice was situated throughout the car to make it cooler and a false ceiling was installed to allow outside air to circulate. Engineers experimented with different running speeds to determine which would cause the least vibration; sixty miles an hour was the agreed-upon number. All other trains were rerouted or held in stations to reduce noise and not delay the presidential party. A national day of prayer was called as businesses closed and special religious services were conducted in America's cities.

Too enervated to talk, Garfield drank just two glasses of beef-tea during the seven-hour journey. Bliss and Agnew monitored his vital signs and, by the end of the exhausting trip, Garfield's heart was racing at almost 125 beats per minute and his temperature had climbed to 101.6. At every one of the forty-six cities, towns, and villages along the train's path, vast crowds thronged the streets. North through Maryland, Delaware, Pennsylvania, and Farmingdale, Freehold, Monmouth Junction, and Sea Girt, the little hamlets that dotted the New Jersey shore, people stood silently, with uncovered heads, hats in their hands, and tears in their eyes. They showed their respect by throwing straw onto the tracks hoping to soften the ride. The Garfields arrived at Elberon shortly after 1 P.M. Starting on the newly laid track, the detached presidential car and its smaller yard engine got stuck going up a slight incline. Several hundred railroad workers streamed forward and used their bare hands to push Garfield's train the last few hundred yards.

In Francklyn Cottage—actually a twenty-room summer mansion, named for its owner, New York financier Charles G. Francklyn—Garfield spent the last two weeks of his life. The sea air did little good as his chills, fever, and vomiting continued unabated, and the beginnings of a worrisome cough, indicative of spreading pneumonia, appeared. Garfield was allowed few visitors—some cabinet officials saw him, but only for a few minutes—never left the cottage, and was barely able to see outside from his second-floor bedroom. "Oh, those windows are so small," Garfield complained to an attendant.[22]

Bliss continued the charade that the president was recovering by dismissing Joseph Barnes, Joseph Woodward, and Robert Reyburn. He defended his action in yet another optimistic medical bulletin, telling the public that Garfield wanted "to relieve them from a labor and responsibility, which in his improved condition he could no longer impose upon them."[23] It was all a prevarication as Bliss and Hamilton maintained promises of a miraculous return to health. Hamilton was even overheard telling another surgeon that "he had the strongest hopes of recovery."[24] Indeed, as Garfield's condition worsened, the daily medical briefings remained sanguine, and government officials even told their counterparts of an expected recovery. "The President's rest was much broken during the first half of last night, but today his condition has been more favorable," Secretary of State Blaine cabled James Russell Lowell, the American minister in London. "His surgeons are much encouraged."[25]

Susan Edson was so incensed by Bliss's deceptions that she departed Elberon. Silas Boynton, the only homeopath left, continued his nursing duties and remained the one source of accurate information for reporters. When Bliss would announce that Garfield had had a favorable day, Boynton countered by telling journalists that the blood poisoning was spreading. Boynton privately advised a correspondent that the president's pulse frequently was over 120, and that knowledge of this unfavorable sign was largely kept from the family and the public. Edson's departure created a reduction in the level of Garfield's nightly nursing care and taxed everyone's patience. In this crisis period, the bulk of the duties were assumed by two of Garfield's old army cronies, Almon Rockwell and David Swaim, neither of whom knew anything about nursing or medicine. A weary Bliss continued his absurdities when he informed reporters, "I am of the opinion that the atmosphere of Long Branch is much better for the President than the atmosphere of Washington. Its influence will be helpful."[26] Coincidentally, a few days earlier, Garfield had pulled Bliss aside. "Doctor, you plainly show the effect of all this care and unrest," whispered the president. "Your anxious watching will soon be over."[27]

On Saturday, September 17, Garfield was prostrated by a severe chill and a hacking cough. For the first time, he complained of a throbbing pain in his chest. Delirious throughout most of the day, Garfield's condition was now considered critical. But none of these developments emerged in Bliss's optimistic communiqués the following day:

Elberon, Long Branch, N.J., September 18, 9:30 A.M.—At the examination of the President at 8:30 A.M., the temperature was 98, pulse 102, respiration 18. . . . The cough was less troublesome than on previous nights, and the expectoration unchanged. He is able to take nourishment and stimulants required, without gastric disturbance, nor has there been evidence of mental aberration during the night.

6 P.M.—The President, though quite weak, has passed a very quiet day. There has been no recurrence of chill nor mental disturbance.[28]

Shortly after 10 P.M. on Monday, September 19, Garfield awoke suddenly and cried out, "Oh, Swaim, this terrible pain," placing his hand over his heart. Swaim offered Garfield a drink of water, but he yelled out again, "Oh, Swaim, this terrible pain. Press your hand on it." Swaim touched his chest and Garfield reflexively threw both his hands up to his side and exclaimed, "Oh, Swaim, can't you stop this?"[29] With that, Garfield fell back on his pillow and became comatose. Swaim sent for Bliss, who was sleeping in the next room. "My God, Swaim, he is dying!" shouted Bliss.[30] The physician, in turn, called for Agnew, Hamilton, and Lucretia. Applying his ear to Garfield's heart, Bliss heard little. This was due to both interference from Garfield's labored breathing and Bliss's disapproval of the recently devised hearing-assistance tube called the stethoscope. At 10:35 P.M., the respirations ceased and Bliss whispered to the assembled, "It is over."[31] Garfield was a few weeks short of his fiftieth birthday.

The shutters of Francklyn Cottage were closed and an American flag, hanging from a pole placed in an upper window, was draped in black. Word of Garfield's death spread rapidly and, in many cities, was announced by the tolling of bells. Vice President Arthur, who was staying at his New York City residence, was informed just before midnight. The transition of power was efficient and grim. A New York Supreme Court justice was located, and, at 2:15 A.M. on September 20, 1881, a shaken Chester A. Arthur was sworn in as the nation's twenty-first president. Several hours later, Arthur left for Elberon to escort Garfield's body back to Washington.

Before Garfield's remains were moved, an autopsy was performed. An embalmer had already injected the corpse with zinc chloride, when, on the afternoon of the twentieth, Agnew, Barnes, Bliss, Hamilton, Reyburn, and Woodward assembled in Garfield's room. They were joined by Daniel S. Lamb, a physician on the staff of the Army Medical Museum in Washington, and Andrew Smith, a local doctor, who was there in case a New Jersey physician's license might be required for legal purposes. Lamb performed the dissection, which revealed that the ball had entered Garfield's body three and a half inches to the right of the spine, fractured the eleventh and twelfth ribs, passed through thoracic and lumbar vertebrae—without injuring the spinal cord—and lodged deep in the tissues of the president's left back, apparently a nonlethal injury. Multiple pus cavities were found, including a massive one that burrowed down into Garfield's right groin—caused by the incessant probing with fingers, surgical instruments, and drainage tubes that planted bacteria wherever they were poked—but not one vital organ was wounded.

"It is quite evident," Bliss and the doctors attested in their autopsy report, "that the different suppurating [pus-producing] surfaces, and especially the fractured spongy tissues of the vertebra, furnish a sufficient explanation of the septic conditions which existed during life."[32] Bliss denied the presence of pyemia—bacteria in the blood—or other findings of major significance. He consigned Garfield's death to the consequences of a broken backbone. No mention was made of antisepsis, germs, pus, or their relationships. When Lamb completed his dissection, the affected vertebrae were removed and brought back to the Army Medical Museum (Garfield's twelfth thoracic and first and second lumbar vertebrae currently reside at the National Museum of Health and Medicine in Washington, D.C.), where they were given to the prosecution for the upcoming trial of Charles Guiteau. Not unexpectedly, Silas Boynton disagreed with the autopsy results. "You say, then, Doctor, that the President had a chance—a reasonable chance—for recovery," asked a reporter, "but that in your opinion these chances were all thrown away by the wretched treatment of the case?" "You express it strongly," answered Boynton, "but you reach a right conclusion."[33] Bliss dismissed Boynton's criticisms, saying, "He [Boynton] seemed disgusted with the whole proceedings."[34]

Garfield's doctors and their supporters would soon be forced to defend their actions and mistaken diagnosis. The recriminations, however, would wait until after the funeral. The day following the autopsy, a train draped in black carried Garfield's body back to Washington. President Arthur and former President Grant accompanied Lucretia and the members of Garfield's cabinet. Bells tolled, flags flew at half-mast, brass bands played funeral dirges, and crowds, several thousand strong, could be found in every town that the train passed through. In Princeton, students lined the tracks with flowers.

Reaching Washington in the late afternoon, Garfield's coffin was placed on a catafalque in the Capitol's massive rotunda. For two days and nights, vast throngs passed by the open coffin, but the sight of the dead president's face was ghastly. "It was pinched and haggard to the last extreme," noted one observer. "The skin yellow and glistening; the eyes shrunken, and the lips tightly drawn. The nose looked unnaturally long, sharp, and hooked; and altogether there was but the slightest resemblance to the heroic form and face of him who had been James A. Garfield."[35] By September 22, signs of decomposition, hastened by the bacteria festering in Garfield's body, set in. The coffin was permanently closed and more flowers placed and perfume sprinkled about the rotunda. Memorial services were conducted on the twenty-third and, later that day, a train containing the coffin and Garfield's immediate family traveled to Cleveland, his final resting place.

10

Aftermath

Charles Guiteau was a wildly successful assassin, not only from the standpoint of murdering a president, but also from the changes that his actions brought to the political arena. None of America's other presidential assassinations so totally fulfilled the shooter's own wishes. Yet, on the first day of Guiteau's trial, a scant two months after Garfield's death, the assassin vehemently opposed the prosecution's attempts to pin the murder on him. "Nothing can be more absurd, because General Garfield died from malpractice," argued Guiteau. "The doctors ought to be indicted for murdering James A. Garfield, and not me." During the ten weeks of his trial, between fits of rage and uncontrollable harangues, and up to the hour of his hanging a year after the shooting, Guiteau relentlessly rehashed the case for medical mistreatment. He debated reporters, shouted out to thousands of courtroom observers, and exasperated his own lawyers, who pursued an insanity defense. Guiteau's syllogism was this: he admitted shooting Garfield, but medical records showed that, three weeks later, a team of physicians conducted a careful examination of the president and concluded he would recover. Two months after this official announcement, following unparalleled treatments, Garfield died. Therefore, according to Guiteau's rationale, "The doctors who mistreated him ought to bear the odium of his death, and not his assailant."[1]

Guiteau was a lunatic with few sane thoughts, but his courtroom utterances about medical malpractice were accurate. His arguments reflected a nationwide brouhaha concerning the medical-legal aspects of Garfield's case. Even Garfield's teenage daughter Mollie commented on the mistreatment: "We all thought darling Papa was on the sure road to recovery, but we were all mistaken . . . the surgeons didn't know anything about the wound."[2] Although doctors were urged not to engage in such bickering—"The best tribute which the medical profession can pay, alike to the memory of our late President and the dignity of the art we practice, will be to avoid all carping criticism on the methods of the medical attendants," wrote one physician editor—these pleas did not stop the condemnation of Bliss's clinical judgments.[3]

Arpad Gerster, a young New York surgeon who would author the country's first surgical textbook based on Listerian principles, noted in his private memoirs that his generation of physicians considered the Garfield case a situation "where ignorance is Bliss."[4] Homeopaths continued their bashing of Bliss: "Is it best for homeopathists to allow this ever self-complacent doctor to hoodwink the public?"[5] Allopaths were, if anything, worse in their condemnation. The physician owner of the widely read *Walsh's Retrospect* said that Bliss did "more to cast distrust upon American surgery than any time heretofore known to our medical history."[6] Bliss's personal ethics were questioned, including whether he manipulated the stock market to his advantage by issuing encouraging reports about the president's condition.

Bliss and his consultant surgeons had many supporters, but there seemed no end to the denunciations, most of which concerned the veracity of the medical bulletins and the treatment of the bullet wound. When John Collins Warren, an influential Harvard surgeon who had studied with Joseph Lister, wrote, "From an antiseptic view, we might criticize the introduction of the finger of several surgeons into the wound . . . these examinations were not in accord with the prevailing present theories," he pressured Garfield's physicians to defend their actions.[7] "Throughout the whole course of the treatment," wrote an angry Hamilton, "contrary to what has been publicly said repeatedly, so far as it was possible to apply the system of antiseptic surgery advocated by Mr. Lister to a wound of this character, it was rigorously employed."[8] Hamilton's response demonstrated the knowledge divide between the older generation of physicians, who regarded Listerism as little more than the dousing of a wound with an antiseptic liquid, and their younger colleagues, who argued that fingers, instruments, and bandages also needed to be antiseptically clean.

The controversies surrounding Garfield's death became a dividing line between the new and the old in American medicine. As the first medical case to be so consistently reported by the lay press and closely followed in the medical journals, the clashes between allopaths and homeopaths and anti- and pro-Listerites highlighted the transition that health care was undergoing. Fueled by the Garfield tragedy, an increasing number of positive articles concerning antisepsis brought about the acceptance of Listerism by the late 1880s. Once this fundamental change occurred, Bliss's defenders resorted to revisionist history to explain Garfield's outcome. In 1894, Robert Reyburn, who touted himself as the last surviving of Garfield's physicians, described how "the most scrupulous cleanliness of the instruments and surgical appliances" was maintained for the president. "It must be remembered that the technique of antiseptic, or more properly speaking aseptic surgery," wrote a defensive Reyburn, "was not so thoroughly appreciated or carried out by operating surgeons in 1881."[9] David Hayes Agnew's biographer offered a similar contention: "The treatment throughout [Garfield's case] was in accord with the rules of the *strictest* antiseptic surgery."[10]

The explanations were little more than rationalizations; Garfield's doctors had continued to use traditional-style medicine at a time when Lister's methods were already well known. As a result of the controversies surrounding the tragedy, the medical profession would have to deal with the embarrassment of the president's death for years to come. Indeed, even following the assassination of William McKinley in 1901, the elders of organized medicine were still defending Garfield's treatment. "Now that the matter is up again for discussion, it should be the duty of medical men, particularly, to set matters and history right, and not encourage the belief, so very general, that President Garfield's wound, fatal in 1881, would be trivial today," wrote a high-ranking official of the American Medical Association. "It was fatal in 1881 and would probably be fatal in 1901."[11]

There was little that was further from the truth. Twenty years earlier, an older generation of American physicians had refused to listen to their younger colleagues about the importance of new ideas, particularly the credibility of Lister's concepts. Despite Bliss, Agnew, and Hamilton's genuine feelings of devotion toward Garfield and their sincere desire to see him get well, this generational divide and the physicians' hubris resulted in the death of an American president. One of Hamilton's assistants explained it best: "Drs. Hamilton and Agnew were old men, and not likely to be pioneers in a new field of surgery."[12]

Americans found other reasons to be angry about Garfield's death. According to an editorial in the respected *Boston Medical and Surgical Journal*, "The absence of trained and experienced nurses from the patient's [Garfield's] bedside has unquestionably excited comment upon the part of many."[13] Nursing schools were first established in 1873 in Boston, New Haven, and New York, and, by 1880, a total of fifteen such institutions were open across the country. Bliss's critics demanded to know why he never brought in trained nurses. Bliss was also attacked for his failure to call in a doctor specializing in pathology—Lamb had little experience in conducting an autopsy—to assist in the postmortem examination. To a wary public, it appeared that Bliss and his team of doctors were unwilling to accept any blame for Garfield's demise.

Other than authoring three articles shortly after the president's death, Bliss rarely commented on the case. In one of his reports, he did offer an apology for making a diagnostic error and assuming that Garfield had been shot in the liver. However, Bliss was quick to challenge his critics to have done any better under the circumstances. "I would ask," wrote Bliss, "whether the conditions could have been improved or mitigated, or his [Garfield's] life preserved longer by any other line of treatment?"[14] Bliss's supporters said his health was broken from the pressures of treating Garfield. An embittered and lonely man, Bliss died in 1889 from heart failure. He left no private papers or diaries: "Much which might be said must remain forever unspoken," was his only explanation.[15] Bliss's second-in-command, Joseph Woodward, provided a starker answer. Following Garfield's death, when the truthfulness of the medical bulletins and the adequacy of the president's care came under public attack, Woodward went into a state of severe mental and physical depression. He spent the last three years of his life in and out of insane asylums until he committed suicide in 1884.

A few years following Garfield's death, a forum was held at the Chicago World's Fair to develop national standards for the organization and administration of America's nursing schools. As a direct result of the conference, a rapid expansion of nursing schools occurred, which allowed tens of thousands of women to join the nation's workforce. Similarly, the trend toward specialization in medicine was spurred by the president's death, as physicians realized the error of not having more specialty-style care available.

Medical malpractice was one thing to argue over, but several months after Garfield's death, when Bliss and six other physicians asked the federal government to compensate them for caring for Garfield, the request became a national scandal. Considering the unprecedented nature and length of Garfield's illness, there were no funds—health insurance did not exist in 1881—from which these unusual claims could be paid. With Bliss and Hamilton each demanding $25,000; Agnew $14,700; Reyburn $10,800; Edson $10,000; Boynton $4,500; and Lamb $1,000, a special appropriations bill was needed. This brought the entire question of Garfield's treatment up for discussion in Congress. "You might as well ask us to use the people's money to pay the doctor's bills of a fourth-class postmaster as those of the President," groused one senator. "They are both paid servants of the people, and if you begin this thing where will it end?"[16]

The physicians' appeals induced scores of other individuals to ask for compensation for services they supposedly performed. From the dozens of yards of expensive calico curtains that Bliss ordered to darken Garfield's room to the tons of ice needed to cool a feverish patient, hundreds of receipts were submitted to Congress. Some of the bills were fraudulent, others unnecessarily inflated, and their presence provoked a bitter controversy. Forced to deal with an extraordinary situation, a special congressional committee met in late 1882 to resolve the monetary issues. Bliss, his team of physicians, and their clinical decision-making prowess were soundly thrashed at public hearings. "The scurrilous attacks of an ignorant politician must be a source of regret to all intelligent persons," countered a physician in an editorial.[17] However, the politicians heard little that was positive about Bliss and, reflecting a growing annoyance with the entire sad episode—particularly the quality of treatment given to Garfield—the audit board limited the doctors to a total of $27,500.[18] Only Boynton received nearly his total request. Bliss was awarded $6,500, and Agnew and Hamilton just $5,000 each.

The tremendous outpouring of grief and adulation occasioned by Garfield's death was short-lived. The Garfield family was supported by a private subscription fund—almost $300,000 was collected nationwide and invested in 4 percent government bonds—organized by Cyrus W. Field, a close friend of the president who headed the Atlantic Telegraph Company, the firm that had successfully laid the first transoceanic telegraph cable. With such largesse, Lucretia gained a measure of financial freedom. She would devote her life to raising her children (of the five who survived into adulthood, the oldest, Harry, would serve a lengthy tenure as president of Williams College, and the second son, James R., would be secretary of the interior in the cabinet of Theodore Roosevelt) and attempting to keep alive the memory of her husband. Eventually, Lucretia would build at Lawnfield—now a National Historic Site— a library wing to hold Garfield's books and papers, establishing a precedent for future presidential libraries.

Despite Lucretia's endeavors regarding her husband's legacy, the efforts would soon prove futile. For several years following his martyrdom, Garfield's life story—one of overcoming adversity, marked self-reliance, and unending hard work—came to exemplify the essence of 1880s America. He was a man of personal contradictions: a scholar turned soldier and a pragmatist turned politician, who proved his inner worth. Through his life story, citizens saw that they could play new roles in a rapidly changing America. In 1887, Lucretia returned to Washington to dedicate an imposing sculpture of Garfield at the foot of Capitol Hill. But, in six short years, memories had already begun to fade and Americans, disappointed with the backbiting antics of their politicians, were looking elsewhere for inspiration. The now-heralded champions were the bankers, businessmen, inventors, labor leaders, scientists, and social activists who provided a socioeconomic dynamism never before seen.

By the 1890s, the Stalwarts and Half-Breeds had disappeared from the political scene and Garfield's brief presidency was forgotten. Usually omitted from even the historical rankings of America's chief executives, Garfield became just another bronze statue or commemorative plaque, frozen in time. His accomplishments as president were few, but the partisan storms during his six months in office and the political reasons for his assassination brought about one of the most far-reaching reforms of the Gilded Age, the Pendleton Civil Service Reform Act of 1883. Taking the first substantive steps to rid the United States civil service of the spoils system, the law established a three-person, bipartisan panel to develop competitive examinations to hire federal employees based on merit rather than politics. It was a fitting memorial to the fallen president.

James Abram Garfield's presidency is reduced to a tantalizing "what if." He was an ambitious elected official who was involved in issues of national importance for almost twenty years. As one of the era's principal Republican congressmen, Garfield helped mold a nascent political party into a force that would lead his country into world leadership. But as a chief executive he was clumsy in controlling his party's factional differences. Garfield was not a natural leader and did not dominate men or events. He was a kindhearted and intelligent individual who was also a calculating politician. Garfield uneasily occupied two worlds, one of ego-driven actions and another of introspection and prudence. Ultimately, it was his lack of assertiveness and worry over the slightest hint of criticism that interfered with his presidential decision making. "I am a poor hater," was Garfield's self-description, and for this reason he is remembered more as a political party functionary—and for having been assassinated—than an inspirational American president.[19]

Epilogue:
Garfield and Modern Medicine

On March 30, 1981, almost one hundred years after James Garfield was assassinated, another president, Ronald Reagan, was shot by a mentally deranged young man. A bullet pierced Reagan's left chest, punctured his lung, and stopped an inch away from his heart and aorta. Bleeding internally and short of breath, he was rushed to the George Washington University Hospital, where he collapsed in the emergency room. Resuscitative measures stabilized Reagan's condition and, within minutes, he was taken into surgery. By the time the three-hour operation ended and the hemorrhage was controlled and the pulmonary injury treated, more than 50 percent of the president's blood volume had been replaced by transfusions. In a tribute to scientific medicine and the recuperative powers of the patient, Reagan was on his feet within twenty-four hours of the shooting and, eleven days later, returned to the White House—fully able to conduct the nation's business. Reagan's wound was much more life-threatening than Garfield's and yet did not kill or even significantly impair him, despite his being twenty years older than Garfield. If Reagan had been shot in 1881, he would have died within hours of the shooting—chest surgery did not exist. How would Garfield have fared if he had received Reagan's level of care?

Garfield likely would have arrived at a medical facility within minutes of the shooting and with an intravenous line already in place. The emergency room doctors would scan an electronically sent electrocardiogram and determine that there were no cardiac abnormalities. A physical examination of Garfield would reveal no obvious pulmonary or abdominal injuries. Since his vital organs were not injured, Garfield's heart and respiratory rates, blood pressure, and blood oxygen level would likely be normal. Similarly, blood tests and urinalysis would be unremarkable. Under no circumstance would the bullet wound be probed or manipulated, but rather would simply be covered with a sterile dressing and left alone.

Since President Garfield was shot in the middle of the right back, X-rays would be taken of the abdomen and chest, demonstrating the presence of the bullet in the left side of his back and two splintered ribs and fractured thoracic and lumbar vertebrae. Everything else would appear normal. To further rule out injuries to structures located along the bullet's path—including the colon, duodenum, kidneys, and pancreas—a high-resolution, computed tomography (CT) scan would be performed and would detail no damage other than what was already known, the bullet embedded deep in the president's back muscles. By this time, ninety minutes would have passed since the assassination attempt, and a fully conscious Garfield would receive pain medicine. The hemorrhage having been moderate in amount, the president would not require transfusions. Garfield would remain in the hospital for observation for the next twenty-four hours and started on antibiotics and not fed as precautionary measures. The following morning, a hungry and relieved Garfield would return to the White House, where he and Lucretia would marvel at the wonders of modern medicine as the president began rehabilitative therapy for his injured spine.

And, in future histories of the Garfield presidency, the assassination attempt would be regarded as a footnote, rather than the whole story.

Notes

1: EARLY YEARS

1. J. S. Ogilvie, *History of the Attempted Assassination of James A. Garfield* (New York: J. S. Ogilvie, 1881), p. 33.
2. *New York Times*, July 3, 1881.
3. Smith Townshend, "President Garfield's Wound and Its Treatment," *Walsh's Retrospect* 2 (1881): 624.
4. Thomas Wolfe, *From Death to Morning* (New York: Charles Scribner's Sons, 1935), p. 121.
5. Theodore C. Smith. *The Life and Letters of James Abram Garfield* (New Haven: Yale University, 1925), vol. 1, p. 5.
6. J. M. Bundy, *The Life of James Abram Garfield* (New York: A. S. Barnes, 1881), p. 13.
7. Smith, *Life and Letters*, p. 16.
8. Ibid., p. 27.
9. Ibid., p. 39.
10. Burke A. Hinsdale, *President Garfield and Education; Hiram College Memorial* (Boston: J. R. Osgood, 1882), p. 32.
11. Harry J. Brown and Frederick D. Williams, eds., *The Diary of James A. Garfield, 1848–1871*, vol. 1 (East Lansing: Michigan State University Press, 1967), pp. 149–50.
12. Quoted in Smith, *Life and Letters*, p. 92.
13. Bundy, *Life of James Abram Garfield*, p. 33.
14. Brown and Williams, *Diary*, p. 267.
15. Ibid., p. 273.
16. Ibid., p. 259.
17. Corydon E. Fuller, *Reminiscences of James A. Garfield* (Cincinnati: Standard Publishing, 1887), p. 236.

18. Smith, *Life and Letters*, p. 109.
19. Fuller, *Reminiscences*, p. 268.
20. Quoted in Smith, *Life and Letters*, p. 151.
21. Quoted in Allan Peskin, *Garfield, A Biography* (Kent, Ohio: Kent State University, 1978), p. 72.
22. William R. Balch, *The Life of James Abram Garfield, Late President of the United States* (Philadelphia: Hubbard Brothers, 1881), p. 107.
23. Brown and Williams, *Diary*, p. 350.
24. Quoted in Peskin, *Garfield, A Biography*, p. 53.
25. John C. Ridpath, *The Life and Work of James A. Garfield* (Cincinnati: Jones Brothers, 1881), p. 85.

2: THE CIVIL WAR

1. Theodore C. Smith, *The Life and Letters of James Abram Garfield* (New Haven: Yale University Press, 1925), vol. 1, p. 160.
2. Quoted in John M. Taylor, *Garfield of Ohio, The Available Man* (New York: W. W. Norton, 1970), p. 65.
3. William R. Balch, *The Life of James Abram Garfield, Late President of the United States* (Philadelphia: Hubbard Brothers, 1881), p. 182.
4. Ibid., p. 171.
5. Smith, *Life and Letters*, p. 224.
6. Ibid., p. 234.
7. Ibid., p. 238.
8. Ibid., p. 246.
9. Ibid., p. 263.
10. Ibid., p. 274.
11. Ibid., p. 275.
12. Ibid., p. 310.
13. Ibid.
14. J. M. Bundy, *The Nation's Hero—In Memoriam: The Life of James Abram Garfield* (New York: A. S. Barnes, 1881), p. 63.
15. Smith, *Life and Letters*, p. 320.
16. Ibid., p. 353.
17. Ibid., p. 356.

3: CONGRESSIONAL CAREER

1. Quoted in Alan Peskin, *Garfield, A Biography* (Kent, Ohio: Kent State University, 1978), p. 230.
2. William R. Balch, *The Life of James Abram Garfield, Late President of the United States* (Philadelphia: Hubbard Brothers, 1881), p. 122.

3. Theodore C. Smith, *The Life and Letters of James Abram Garfield*, vol. 1 (New Haven: Yale University Press, 1925), p. 266.
4. Ibid., p. 376.
5. Ibid., p. 378.
6. Ibid., p. 379.
7. John Shaw, ed., *Crete and James, Personal Letters of Lucretia and James Garfield* (East Lansing: Michigan State University Press, 1994), p. 218.
8. Burke A. Hinsdale, *The Works of James Abram Garfield*, vol. 1 (Boston: James R. Osgood, 1882), p. 86.
9. Smith, *Life and Letters*, p. 425.
10. Ibid., p. 426.
11. Hinsdale, *Works*, vol. 2, p. 97.
12. Ibid., vol. 1, p. 208.
13. Smith, *Life and Letters*, pp. 466–67.
14. Hinsdale, *Works*, vol. 2, p. 2.
15. Smith, *Life and Letters*, p. 450.
16. Ibid.
17. *New York Tribune*, February 19, 1873.
18. Harry J. Brown and Frederick D. Williams, eds., *The Diary of James A. Garfield, 1872–1874*, vol. 2 (East Lansing: Michigan State University Press, 1967), p. 138.
19. Smith, *Life and Letters*, p. 548.
20. Russell H. Conwell, *The Life, Speeches, and Public Services of James A. Garfield* (Portland, Maine: George Stinson, 1881), p. 312.
21. Brown and Williams, *Diary*, p. 271.
22. Quoted in John M. Taylor, *Garfield of Ohio, The Available Man* (New York: W. W. Norton, 1970), p. 148.
23. Smith, *Life and Letters*, p. 567.
24. Quoted in Taylor, *Garfield of Ohio*, p. 149.
25. Smith, *Life and Letters*, p. 575.
26. Ibid., p. 581.
27. Ibid., p. 602.
28. Quoted in Peskin, *Garfield, A Biography*, p. 411.
29. Ibid., p. 417.
30. Smith, *Life and Letters*, p. 641.
31. Brown and Williams, *Diary*, vol. 3, *1875–1877*, p. 458.
32. Ibid., vol. 4, *1878–1881*, p. 32.
33. Ibid.

4: THE PRIVATE GARFIELD

1. Theodore C. Smith, *The Life and Letters of James Abram Garfield,* vol. 2 (New Haven: Yale University Press, 1925), p. 918.
2. John Shaw, ed., *Crete and James, Personal Letters of Lucretia and James Garfield* (East Lansing: Michigan State University Press, 1994), p. 237.
3. Ibid., p. 255.
4. Quoted in Harry J. Brown and Frederick D. Williams, eds., *The Diary of James A Garfield, 1848–1871,* vol. 1 (East Lansing: Michigan State University Press, 1967), p. 1.
5. Ibid., p. 250.
6. Quoted in Margaret Leech and Harry J. Brown, *The Garfield Orbit* (New York: Harper & Row, 1978), p. 188.
7. Smith, *Life and Letters,* p. 918.
8. William R. Balch, *The Life of James Abram Garfield, Late President of the United States* (Philadelphia: Hubbard Brothers, 1881), p. 332.
9. Smith, *Life and Letters,* p. 746.
10. James G. Blaine, *James A. Garfield, Memorial Address Pronounced in the Hall of Representatives* (Washington, D.C.: Government Printing Office, 1882), p. 29.
11. Brown and Williams, *Diary, 1875–1877,* vol. 3, p. 402.
12. John Sherman, *Recollections of Forty Years in the House, Senate and Cabinet, An Autobiography,* vol. 2 (Chicago: Werner, 1895), p. 807.
13. Quoted in Caroline T. Harnsberger, ed., *Treasury of Presidential Quotations* (Chicago: Follet, 1964), p. 273.
14. Smith, *Life and Letters,* p. 526.

5: THE PRESIDENTIAL ELECTION OF 1880

1. Theodore C. Smith, *The Life and Letters of James Abram Garfield,* vol. 2 (New Haven: Yale University Press, 1925), p. 953.
2. Ibid., p. 951.
3. Harry J. Brown and Frederick D. Williams, eds., *The Diary of James A. Garfield, 1878–1881,* vol. 4 (East Lansing: Michigan State University Press, 1981), p. 411.
4. John Shaw, ed., *Crete and James, Personal Letters of Lucretia and James Garfield* (East Lansing: Michigan State University Press, 1994), p. 374.
5. Ibid., p. 371.
6. Smith, *Life and Letters,* p. 967.
7. Ibid., p. 971.

8. William R. Balch, *The Life of James Abram Garfield, Late President of the United States* (Philadelphia: Hubbard Brothers, 1881), p. 403.
9. Smith, *Life and Letters*, p. 972.
10. Quoted in Kenneth D. Ackerman, *Dark Horse: The Surprise Election and Political Murder of President James A. Garfield* (New York: Carroll & Graf, 2003), p. 84.
11. Quoted in John C. Ridpath, *The Life and Work of James A. Garfield* (Cincinnati: Jones Brothers, 1881), pp. 431–32.
12. Burke A. Hinsdale, ed., *The Works of James Abram Garfield*, vol. 2 (Boston: James R. Osgood, 1883), pp. 778–79.
13. Smith, *Life and Letters*, p. 976.
14. Ibid., pp. 981–82
15. Shaw, *Crete and James*, p. 377.
16. Smith, *Life and Letters*, p. 990.
17. Quoted in *Encyclopaedia Britannica*, 13th ed., "William Learned Marcy."
18. Hinsdale, *Works*, p. 786.
19. Brown and Williams, *Diary*, p. 430.
20. Ibid., p. 439.
21. Smith, *Life and Letters*, p. 1028.
22. Hinsdale, *Works*, p. 785.
23. Smith, *Life and Letters*, p. 1039.
24. Ibid., p. 1043.
25. John Sherman, *Recollections of Forty Years in the House, Senate and Cabinet, An Autobiography*, vol. 2 (Chicago: Werner, 1895), p. 789.

6: GARFIELD'S ADMINISTRATION

1. Quoted in Robert G. Caldwell, *James A. Garfield, Party Chieftain* (New York: Dodd, Mead & Co., 1931), p. 301.
2. Harry J. Brown and Frederick D. Williams, eds., *The Diary of James A. Garfield, 1878–1881*, vol. 4 (East Lansing: Michigan State University Press, 1981), p. 435.
3. Quoted in Gail Hamilton, *Biography of James G. Blaine* (Norwich, Conn.: Henry Bill Publishing, 1895), pp. 490–91.
4. Ibid., p. 495.
5. Ibid., pp. 495–96.
6. Brown and Williams, *Diary*, pp. 506–7.
7. Theodore C. Smith, *The Life and Letters of James Abram Garfield*, vol. 2 (New Haven: Yale University Press, 1925), pp. 1056–57.
8. Ibid., p. 1078.

9. Brown and Williams, *Diary*, p. 530.
10. Ibid., p. 552.
11. Quoted in Smith, *Life and Letters*, p. 1093.
12. Brown and Williams, *Diary*, p. 554.
13. Theron C. Crawford, *James G. Blaine, A Study of His Life and Career* (n.p.: Edgewood Publishing, 1893), p. 495.
14. Brown and Williams, *Diary*, p. 512.
15. Ibid., p. 544.
16. Caldwell, *James A. Garfield*, p. 330.
17. John C. Ridpath, *The Life and Work of James A. Garfield* (Cincinnati: Jones Brothers, 1881), p. 489.
18. Ibid., p. 491.
19. Ibid., pp. 492, 493, 495.
20. Brown and Williams, *Diary*, p. 555.
21. H. H. Alexander, *The Life of Guiteau and The Official History of The Most Exciting Case on Record: Being The Trial of Guiteau for Assassinating Pres. Garfield* (Philadelphia: National Publishing, 1882), p. 94.
22. H. G. Hayes and C. J. Hayes, *A Complete History of the Trial of Guiteau, Assassin of President Garfield* (Philadelphia: Hubbard Brothers, 1882), p. 57.
23. Brown and Williams, *Diary*, p. 569.
24. Ibid., p. 610.
25. Smith, *Life and Letters*, p. 1167.
26. Ibid., p. 1158.
27. Brown and Williams, *Diary*, p. 561.
28. Smith, *Life and Letters*, p. 1083.
29. Quoted in John M. Taylor, *Garfield of Ohio, The Available Man* (New York: W. W. Norton, 1970), p. 243.
30. Smith, *Life and Letters*, p. 1109.
31. Quoted in ibid., p. 1119.
32. Quoted in ibid.
33. Brown and Williams, *Diary*, p. 608.
34. Ibid., p. 597.
35. Quoted in ibid., *1848–1871*, vol. 1, p. lxiii.
36. Alexander, *Life of Guiteau*, p. 97.
37. Brown and Williams, *Diary*, p. 609.
38. Ibid.
39. Ibid., p. 589.
40. Hayes and Hayes, *Complete History of the Trial of Guiteau*, p. 431.

7: THE ASSASSINATION ATTEMPT

1. *New York Times*, July 3, 1881.
2. J. S. Ogilvie, *The Life and Death of James A. Garfield* (New York: J. S. Ogilvie, 1881), p. 34.
3. Ibid., p. 35.
4. H. H. Alexander, *The Life of Guiteau and The Official History of The Most Exciting Case on Record: Being The Trial of Guiteau for Assassinating Pres. Garfield* (Philadelphia: National Publishing, 1882), p. 47.
5. D. W. Bliss, "Report of the Case of President Garfield, Accompanied with a Detailed Account of the Autopsy," *Medical Record* 20 (1881): 393.
6. Ibid.
7. John C. Ridpath, *The Life and Work of James A. Garfield, and The Tragic Story of His Death* (Cincinnati: Jones Brothers, 1881), p. 520.
8. *New York Times*, July 3, 1881.
9. Quoted in ibid.
10. Ibid.
11. Ogilvie, *Life and Death*, p. 43.
12. *New York Times*, July 3, 1881.
13. Ibid.
14. Robert Reyburn, "Clinical History of the Case of President James Abram Garfield," *Journal of the American Medical Association* 22 (1894): 413.
15. Ibid.
16. Philip S. Wales, "President Garfield's Wound and Its Treatment," *Walsh's Retrospect* 2 (1881): 628.
17. Ridpath, *Life and Work*, pp. 522–23.
18. D. W. Bliss, "The Story of President Garfield's Illness," *Century Magazine* 23 (1881): 300.
19. Wales, "President Garfield's Wound," p. 628.
20. Quoted in Kenneth D. Ackerman, *Dark Horse: The Surprise Election and Political Murder of President James A. Garfield* (New York: Carroll & Graf, 2003), pp. 402–3.
21. Ibid., p. 403.
22. *New York Times*, July 5, 1881.
23. Wales, "President Garfield's Wound," p. 628.
24. William R. Balch, *Life of James Abram Garfield, Late President of the United States* (Philadelphia: Hubbard Brothers, 1881), p. 599.
25. Bliss, "Report of the Case of President Garfield," p. 395.
26. *New York Times*, July 5, 1881.
27. Ridpath, *Life and Work*, pp. 535, 555.

8: THE STATE OF AMERICAN MEDICINE

1. Anon., "Remarks on Medical Fees," *New York Monthly Chronicle of Medicine and Surgery* 1 (1824–1825): 25.
2. T. Dwight Stowe, "Treatment of President Garfield," *Homoeopathic Physician* 1 (1881): 534–35.
3. Susan Edson, "The Sickness and Nursing of President Garfield with Many Interesting Incidents Never Before Given to the Public," in William R. Balch, *Life of President Garfield* (Philadelphia: Hubbard Brothers, 1881), p. 614.
4. Ruth S.-B. Feis, *Mollie Garfield in the White House* (Chicago: Rand McNally, 1963), p. 71.
5. *New York Sun*, July 16, 1881.
6. Robert Reyburn, "Clinical History of the Case of President James Abram Garfield," *Journal of the American Medical Association* 22 (1894): 463.
7. Edson, "Sickness and Nursing," p. 619.
8. Anon., "The Evidence," *Walsh's Retrospect* 3 (1882): 305–7.
9. Silas Boynton, "President Garfield's Case," *American Observer Medical Monthly* 18 (1881): 493.
10. Thomas H. Sherman, *Twenty Years with James G. Blaine: Reminiscences by His Private Secretary* (New York: Grafton Press, 1928), p. 88.
11. William Williams Keen, "Military Surgery in 1861 and in 1918," *Annals of the American Academy of Political and Social Science* 80 (1918): 18.
12. George Shrady, "The New York Hospital," editorial, *Medical Record* 13 (1878): 113.
13. D. W. Bliss, "Report of the Case of President Garfield, Accompanied with a Detailed Account of the Autopsy," *Medical Record* 20 (1881): 399.
14. John Ashhurst, Jr., ed., *Transactions of the International Medical Congress of Philadelphia* (Philadelphia: Printed for the Congress, 1877), p. 517.
15. Anon., "Letter from Philadelphia," *Boston Medical and Surgical Journal* 95 (1876): 366.
16. Frank H. Hamilton, in Ashhurst, *Transactions*, p. 532.
17. Edward H. Clarke, Henry J. Bigelow, Samuel D. Gross et al., *A Century of American Medicine, 1776–1876* (Philadelphia: Henry C. Lea, 1876), p. 213.
18. Joseph Lister, "The Antiseptic Method of Dressing Open Wounds," *Medical Record* 11 (1876): 696.
19. James D. McCabe, *The Life and Public Services of Gen. James A. Garfield* (Tecumseh, Mich.: A. W. Mills, 1881), p. 591.

20. Reyburn, "Clinical History," p. 460.
21. Ibid.
22. John C. Ridpath, *The Life and Work of James A. Garfield* (Cincinnati: Jones Brothers, 1881), p. 540.
23. D. W. Bliss, "The Story of President Garfield's Illness," *Century Magazine* 23 (1881): 304.
24. Theodore C. Smith, *The Life and Letters of James Abram Garfield* (New Haven: Yale University Press, 1925), vol. 2, p. 1193.
25. Ridpath, *Life and Work*, p. 552.
26. Reyburn, "Clinical History," pp. 463–64.
27. Boynton, "President Garfield's Case," p. 493.
28. Reyburn, "Clinical History," p. 464.

9: EIGHTY DAYS

1. John C. Ridpath, *The Life and Work of James A. Garfield* (Cincinnati: Jones Brothers, 1881), p. 562.
2. W. H. Dukeman, "The President's Wound," *Medical Record* 20 (1881): 139.
3. Frank Baker, "President Garfield's Case, A Diagnosis Made July 4th," *Walsh's Retrospect* 2 (1881): 621.
4. Quoted in Kenneth D. Ackerman, *Dark Horse: The Surprise Election and Political Murder of President James A. Garfield* (New York, Carroll & Graf, 2003), p. 411.
5. Quoted in James C. Clark, *The Murder of James A. Garfield, The President's Last Days and the Trial and Execution of his Assassin* (Jefferson N.C.: McFarland, 1993), p. 86.
6. Robert Reyburn, "Clinical History of the Case of President James Abram Garfield," *Journal of the American Medical Association* 22 (1894): 500.
7. Ridpath, *Life and Work*, p. 571.
8. Alexander G. Bell, "Upon the Electrical Experiments to Determine the Location of the Bullet in the Body of the Late President Garfield: and Upon a Successful Form of Induction Balance for the Painless Detection of Metallic Masses in the Human Body," *American Journal of Science* 25 (1883): 50.
9. Quoted in Clark, *Murder of James A. Garfield*, p. 115.
10. Ridpath, *Life and Work*, p. 578.
11. Robert Reyburn, "The Case of President James A. Garfield: An Abstract of the Clinical History," *American Medicine* 2 (1901): 500.
12. Theodore C. Smith, *The Life and Letters of James Abram Garfield* (New Haven: Yale University Press, 1925), vol. 2, p. 1196.
13. Ridpath, *Life and Work*, p. 581.

14. Albert G. Riddle, *The Life, Character and Public Service of James A. Garfield* (Cleveland: W. W. Williams, 1882), p. 534.
15. Ridpath, *Life and Work*, p. 625.
16. Reyburn, "Clinical History," p. 415.
17. Anon., "The President's Case," editorial, *Gaillard's Medical Journal* 32 (1881): 189.
18. *New York Daily Tribune*, August 17, 1881.
19. Ridpath, *Life and Work*, p. 573.
20. Reyburn, "Clinical History," pp. 581–82.
21. Ridpath, *Life and Work*, p. 618.
22. Ibid., p. 624.
23. Reyburn, "Clinical History," p. 622.
24. Ridpath, *Life and Work*, p. 627.
25. Ibid.
26. James D. McCabe, *The Life and Public Services of Gen. James A. Garfield* (Tecumseh, Mich.: A. W. Mills, 1881), p. 663.
27. Reyburn, "Clinical History," p. 624.
28. Anon., "Official Bulletins of the President's Case," *Boston Medical and Surgical Journal* 105 (1881): 304.
29. McCabe, *Life and Public Services*, p. 684.
30. Ibid., p. 685.
31. Reyburn, "Clinical History," p. 665.
32. D. W. Bliss, J. K. Barnes, J. J. Woodward et al., "Record of the Post-Mortem Examination of the Body of President J. A. Garfield, Made September 20, 1881, Commencing at 4:30 P.M., Eighteen Hours After Death, At Francklyn Cottage, Elberon, New Jersey," *American Journal of the Medical Sciences* 164 (1881): 590.
33. Silas Boynton, "President Garfield's Case," *American Observer Medical Monthly* 18 (1881): 492.
34. Quoted in Clark, *Murder of James A. Garfield*, p. 112.
35. Ridpath, *Life and Work*, p. 656.

10: AFTERMATH

1. R. H. Alexander, *The Life of Guiteau and The Official History of the Most Exciting Case on Record: Being The Trial of Guiteau* (Philadelphia: National Publishing, 1881), p. 138.
2. Ruth S.-B. Feis, *Mollie Garfield in the White House* (Chicago: Rand McNally, 1963), p. 94.
3. George F. Shrady, "The End at Last," *Medical Record* 20 (1881): 350.
4. Arpad G. Gerster, *Recollections of a New York Surgeon* (New York: Paul B. Hoeber, 1917), p. 206 (annotated copy in author's collection).

5. R. W. Conant, "Dr. Bliss' 'Greatest Triumph,'" *Medical Counselor* 6 (1881): 89.
6. Ralph Walsh, "President Garfield's Wound and Its Treatment," *Walsh's Retrospect* 2 (1881): 633.
7. John C. Warren, "Case of President Garfield," *Boston Medical and Surgical Journal* 105 (1881): 464.
8. Frank H. Hamilton, "The Case of President Garfield," *Medical Gazette* 8 (1881): 334.
9. Robert Reyburn, "Clinical History of the Case of President James Abram Garfield," *Journal of the American Medical Association* 22 (1894): 416.
10. J. Howe Adams, *History of the Life of D. Hayes Agnew, M.D., LL.D.* (Philadelphia: F. A. Davis, 1892), p. 240.
11. Anon., "Death of President McKinley," *Journal of the American Medical Association* 37 (1901): 780.
12. John H. Girdner, "The Death of President Garfield," *Munsey's Magazine* 26 (1902): 547.
13. Anon., "The President's Wound, and the Management of the Case," editorial, *Boston Medical and Surgical Journal* 105 (1881): 309.
14. D. W. Bliss, "Report of the Case of President Garfield, Accompanied with a Detailed Account of the Autopsy," *Medical Record* 20 (1881): 399.
15. D. W. Bliss, "The Story of President Garfield's Illness," *Century Magazine* 23 (1881): 305.
16. Quoted in Girdner, "Death of President Garfield," p. 549.
17. Anon., "The Fees of the Medical Advisers of President Garfield," editorial, *Medical News* 41 (1882): 41.
18. W. Lawrence, W. W. Upton, and J. Gilfillan, "Expenses of President Garfield's Illness and Death," Miscellaneous Document 14, 47th Cong., House of Representatives, 2nd sess., January 2, 1883, pp. 1–12.
19. Harry J. Brown and Frederick D. Williams, *The Diary of James A. Garfield, 1875–1877*, vol. 3 (East Lansing: Michigan State University Press, 1973), p. 281.

Milestones

1831   Born in Orange, Ohio, on November 19

1833   Garfield's father, Abram Garfield, dies in May

1848   Leaves home to work on a canal boat

1849–50   Attends Geauga Academy in Chester, Ohio

1851–54   Enrolled at Western Reserve Eclectic Institute in Hiram, Ohio

1854–56   Matriculates at Williams College in Williamstown, Massachusetts

1856   Returns to Ohio to teach at Western Reserve Eclectic Institute (now Hiram College)

1858   Marries Lucretia Rudolph in November

1859   Elected as youngest member to the Ohio senate

1860   First child is born; admitted to Ohio bar

1861   Commissioned a lieutenant colonel in the United States Army

1862   Masterminds campaign to drive Confederate soldiers from the Big Sandy Valley in eastern Kentucky; promoted to brigadier general; elected as a Republican to the U.S. Congress in November

1863   Battle of Chickamauga and ride through enemy lines; enters Congress in December

1864   Reelected to U.S. Congress following the "I must go as a free man" speech

1867–69 Chairman, Committee on Military Affairs

1869–71 Chairman, Committee on Banking and Currency

1871–75 Chairman, Committee on Appropriations

1872–73 Crédit Mobilier scandal

1874   DeGolyer-McClelland contract scandal

1876   Member of special congressional Electoral Commission to resolve presidential election impasse

1878   Recognized as the ranking House Republican

1880   Elected to the United States Senate; elected president of the United States

1881   Inaugurated on March 4; shot by Charles Julius Guiteau on July 2; lingers for two and a half months and dies at Elberon, New Jersey, on September 19; interred on September 26 at Lake View Cemetery, Cleveland, Ohio

Bibliography

BOOKS

Ackerman, Kenneth D. *Dark Horse: The Surprise Election and Political Murder of President James A. Garfield.* New York: Carroll & Graf, 2003.

Adams, J. Howe. *History of the Life of D. Hayes Agnew, M.D., LL.D.* Philadelphia: F. A. Davis, 1892.

Alexander, H. H. *The Life of Guiteau and The Official History of the Most Exciting Case on Record: Being The Trial of Guiteau for Assassinating Pres. Garfield.* Philadelphia: National, 1882.

Alger, Horatio. *From Canal Boy to President, or the Boyhood and Manhood of James A. Garfield.* New York: John R. Anderson, 1881.

Ashhurst, John. *Transactions of the International Medical Congress of Philadelphia, 1876.* Philadelphia: For the Congress, 1877.

Balch, William R. *The Life of James Abram Garfield, Late President of the United States.* Philadelphia: Hubbard Bros., 1881.

Barnard, Harry. *Rutherford B. Hayes and His America.* Indianapolis: Bobbs-Merrill, 1954.

Beale, Harriet S. Blaine. *Letters of Mrs. James G. Blaine.* 2 vols. New York: Duffield, 1908.

Blaine, James G. *James A. Garfield, Memorial Address.* Washington, D.C.: Government Printing Office, 1882.

Boyd, James P. *Life and Public Service of Hon. James G. Blaine, The Illustrious American Orator, Diplomat and Statesman.* Philadelphia: Publishers Union, 1893.

Brieger, Gert H. *Medical America in the Nineteenth Century.* Baltimore: Johns Hopkins Press, 1972.

Brooks, Stewart M. *Our Murdered Presidents: The Medical Story.* New York: Frederick Fell, 1966.

Brown, E. E. *The Life and Public Services of James A. Garfield.* Boston: D. L. Guernsey, 1881.

Brown, Harry J., and Frederick D. Williams. *The Diary of James A. Garfield.* 4 vols. East Lansing: Michigan State University, 1967, 1973, 1981.

Bundy, J. M. *The Life of James Abram Garfield: With An Account of the President's Death and Funeral Obsequies.* New York: A. S. Barnes, 1881.

Bunting III, Josiah. *Ulysses S. Grant.* New York: Times Books/Henry Holt, 2004.

Caldwell, Robert G. *James Garfield, Party Chieftain.* New York: Dodd, Mead, 1931.

Calhoun, Charles W., ed. *The Gilded Age: Essays on the Origins of Modern America.* Wilmington, Del.: Scholarly Resources, 1996.

Cashman, Sean D. *America in the Gilded Age.* New York: New York University Press, 1993.

Chidsey, Donald. *Gentleman from New York: A Life of Roscoe Conkling.* New Haven: Yale University, 1935.

Clancy, Herbert J. *The Presidential Election of 1880.* Chicago: Loyola University Press, 1958.

Clark, James C. *The Murder of James A. Garfield: The President's Last Days and the Trial and Execution of His Assassin.* Jefferson, N.C.: McFarland, 1994.

Clemmer, Mary. *Ten Years in Washington: Or, Inside Life and Scenes in Our National Capital as a Woman Sees Them.* Hartford, Conn.: Hartford, 1882.

Complete Medical Record of President Garfield's Case, Containing All of the Official Bulletins, From the Day of the Shooting to the Day of His Death, Together With the Official Autopsy, Made September 20, 1881, And a Diagram Showing the Course Taken By the Ball; Compiled From the Records of the Executive Mansion. Washington, D.C.: C. A. Wimer, 1881.

Conkling, Alfred R. *Life and Letters of Roscoe Conkling.* New York: Charles L. Webster, 1889.

Conwell, Russell H. *The Life, Speeches, and Public Services of James A. Garfield, Including An Account of his Assassination, Lingering Pain, Death, and Burial.* Portland, Maine: George Stinson, 1881.

Coulter, John. *Our Martyr Presidents, Lincoln: Garfield: McKinley.* n.p.: Memorial, 1901.

Crapol, Edward P. *James G. Blaine: Architect of Empire.* Wilmington, Del.: Scholarly Resources, 2000.

Crawford, Theron C. *James G. Blaine, A Study of His Life and Career.* n.p.: Edgewood, 1893.

Davison, Kenneth E. *The Presidency of Rutherford B. Hayes.* Westport, Conn.: Greenwood, 1972.

Doenecke, Justus D. *The Presidencies of James A. Garfield & Chester A. Arthur.* Lawrence: University of Kansas, 1981.

Excerpts From Opinions of the Distinguished Medical Men and Other Countries Justify the Treatment of the Late President Garfield, Together With a Letter in Reply to the Resolution of the Special Committee of the House of Representatives Referring to the Expenses Consequent Upon His Illness and Death. Washington, D.C.: Gibson Brothers, 1882.

Farmer, Laurence. *Master Surgeon, A Biography of Joseph Lister.* New York: Harper & Row, 1962.

Feis, Ruth S.-B. *Mollie Garfield in the White House.* Chicago: Rand McNally, 1963.

Fisher, Richard B. *Joseph Lister, 1827–1912.* New York: Stein & Day, 1977.

Fuller, Corydon E. *Reminiscences of James A. Garfield.* Cincinnati: Standard, 1887.

Gaw, Jerry L. *"A Time to Heal": The Diffusion of Listerism in Victorian Britain.* Philadelphia: American Philosophical Society, 1999.

Geary, Rick. *The Fatal Bullet.* New York: NBM, 1999.

Gems of Poetry and Song on James A. Garfield. Columbus, Ohio: J. C. McClenahan, 1881.

Gevitz, Norman. *Other Healers, Unorthodox Medicine in America.* Baltimore: Johns Hopkins Press, 1988.

Godlee, Rickman J. *Lord Lister.* Oxford: Clarendon, 1924.

Goebel, Dorothy B., and Julius Goebel. *Generals in the White House.* Garden City, N.Y.: Doubleday, Doran, 1945.

Guthrie, Douglas. *Lord Lister: His Life and Doctrine.* Edinburgh: E. & S. Livingstone, 1949.

Haller, John S. *American Medicine in Transition, 1840–1910.* Urbana: University of Illinois, 1981.

Hamilton, Gail. *Biography of James G. Blaine.* Norwich, Conn.: Henry Bill, 1895.

Hart, Albert B. *Salmon Portland Chase.* Boston: Houghton Mifflin, 1899.

Hayes, H. G., and C. J. Hayes. *A Complete History of the Trial of Guiteau, Assassin of President Garfield.* Philadelphia: Hubbard Bros., 1882.

Hinsdale, Burke A. *The Works of James Abram Garfield.* 2 vols. Boston: James R. Osgood, 1882, 1883.

Hoogenboom, Ari. *Outlawing the Spoils: A History of the Civil Service Reform Movement, 1865–1883.* Urbana: University of Illinois, 1961.

————. *The Presidency of Rutherford B. Hayes.* Lawrence: University of Kansas, 1988.

————. *Rutherford B. Hayes: Warrior and President.* Lawrence: University of Kansas, 1995.

Howe, George. *Chester A. Arthur: A Quarter-Century of Machine Politics.* New York: Dodd, Mead, 1934.

Hoyt, Edwin P. *James A. Garfield.* Chicago: Reilly & Lee, 1964.

Index to the James A. Garfield Papers. Washington, D.C.: Library of Congress, 1973.

Jordan, David M. *Roscoe Conkling of New York: Voice in the Senate.* Ithaca, N.Y.: Cornell University, 1971.

Karabell, Zachary. *Chester Alan Arthur.* New York: Times Books/Henry Holt, 2004.

Kaufman, Martin. *Homeopathy in America.* Baltimore: Johns Hopkins University Press, 1971.

Kingsbury, Robert. *The Assassination of James A. Garfield.* New York: Rosen, 2002.

Leech, Margaret, and Harry J. Brown. *The Garfield Orbit.* New York: Harper & Row, 1978.

MacMahon, Edward B., and Leonard Curry. *Medical Cover-Ups in the White House.* Washington, D.C.: Farragut, 1987.

McCabe, James D. *The Life and Public Services of Gen. James A. Garfield, Our Martyred President.* Tecumseh, Mich.: A. W. Mills, 1881.

McClure, J. B. *Gen. Garfield, From the Log Cabin to the White House.* Chicago: Rhodes & McClure, 1881.

Morgan, H. Wayne. *The Gilded Age, A Reappraisal.* Syracuse, N.Y.: Syracuse University, 1963.

Muzzey, David S. *James G. Blaine: A Political Idol of Other Days.* New York: Dodd, Mead, 1934.

Northrop, Henry D. *Life and Public Services of Hon. James G. Blaine.* Bangor, Maine: Standard Books, 1893.

Norton, Marcus P., and Lewis C. Lillie. *Memorial Services In Honor of James Abram Garfield, Held At Sea, On the Cunard Steamship "Scythia," September 26, 1881.* Boston: Franklin Press, 1882.

Ogilvie, J. S. *History of the Attempted Assassination of James A. Garfield.* New York: J. S. Ogilvie, 1881.

————. *The Life and Death of James A. Garfield.* New York: J. S. Ogilvie, 1881.

Perry, James M. *Touched With Fire, Five Presidents and the Civil War Battles That Made Them.* New York: Public Affairs, 2003.

Peskin, Allan. *Garfield, A Biography.* Kent, Ohio: Kent State University, 1978.

Pessen, Edward. *The Log Cabin Myth: The Social Backgrounds of the Presidents.* New Haven: Yale University, 1984.

Pletcher, David M. *The Awkward Years: American Foreign Relations Under Garfield and Arthur.* Columbia: University of Missouri, 1962.

Reeves, Thomas. *Gentleman Boss: The Life and Times of Chester Alan Arthur.* Newton, Conn.: American Political Biography, 1975.

Reid, J. A., and R. A. Reid. *Garfield's Career: From the Tow-Path to the White House; His Seventy-Nine Days' Struggle for Life, and the Public Obsequies.* Providence, R.I.: J. A. & R. A. Reid, 1881.

Report of the Proceedings in the Case of the United States vs. Charles J. Guiteau, Tried in the Supreme Court of the District of Columbia, Holding a Criminal Term, and Beginning November 14, 1881. 3 vols. Washington, D.C.: Government Printing Office, 1882.

Reverby, Susan M. *Ordered to Care, The Dilemma of American Nursing, 1850–1945.* Cambridge: Cambridge University Press, 1987.

Riddle, Albert G. *The Life, Character and Public Service of James A. Garfield.* Cleveland: W. W. Williams, 1880.

Ridpath, John C. *The Life and Work of James A. Garfield, and the Tragic Story of his Death.* Cincinnati: Jones Brothers, 1881.

Roberts, Mary M. *American Nursing, History and Interpretation.* New York: Macmillan, 1954.

Rosenberg, Charles E. *The Trial of the Assassin Guiteau, Psychiatry and Law in the Gilded Age.* Chicago: University of Chicago, 1968.

Rothstein, William G. *American Physicians in the Nineteenth Century, From Sects to Science.* Baltimore: Johns Hopkins University Press, 1972.

Rupp, Robert O., ed. *James A. Garfield, A Bibliography.* Westport, Conn.: Greenwood, 1997.

Russell, Charles E. *Blaine of Maine: His Life and Times.* New York: Cosmopolitan Book, 1931.

Rutkow, Ira M. *The History of Surgery in the United States, 1775–1900,* vol. 1, *Textbooks, Monographs & Treatises.* San Francisco: Norman, 1988.

———. *The History of Surgery in the United States, 1775–1900,* vol. 2, *Periodicals & Pamphlets.* San Francisco: Norman, 1992.

———. *Surgery: An Illustrated History.* St. Louis, Mo.: Mosby-YearBook, 1993.

———. *American Surgery: An Illustrated History.* Philadelphia: Lippincott-Raven, 1998.

———. *Bleeding Blue and Gray: Civil War Surgery and the Evolution of American Medicine.* New York: Random House, 2005.

Shaw, John, ed. *Crete and James, Personal Letters of Lucretia and James Garfield.* East Lansing: Michigan State University, 1994.

Sherman, John. *Recollections of Forty Years in the House, Senate and Cabinet, An Autobiography.* 2 vols. Chicago: Werner, 1895.

Sherman, Thomas H. *Twenty Years with James G. Blaine: Reminiscences by His Private Secretary.* New York: Grafton, 1928.

Shryock, Richard H. *Medicine in America, Historical Essays.* Baltimore: Johns Hopkins University Press, 1966.

Smith, Theodore C. *The Life and Letters of James Abram Garfield.* 2 vols. New Haven: Yale University, 1925.

Taylor, John M. *Garfield of Ohio, The Available Man.* New York: W. W. Norton, 1970.

Thayer, William M. *From Log-Cabin to White House, Life of James A. Garfield.* Boston: James H. Earle, 1881.

Trefousse, Hans L. *Rutherford B. Hayes.* New York: Times Books/Henry Holt, 2002.

Truax, Rhoda. *Joseph Lister, Father of Modern Surgery.* Indianapolis: Bobbs-Merrill, 1944.

Turner, A. Logan. *Joseph, Baron Lister, Centenary Volume, 1827–1927.* Edinburgh: Oliver & Boyd, 1927.

Tutorow, Norman E. *James Gillespie Blaine and the Presidency.* New York: Peter Lang, 1989.

U.S. Navy Department. *Reports of Officers of the Navy on Ventilating and Cooling the Executive Mansion During the Illness of President Garfield.* Washington, D.C.: Government Printing Office, 1882.

Warden, Robert B. *An Account of the Private Life and Public Services of Salmon Portland Chase.* Cincinnati: Wilstach, Baldwin, 1874.

Wrench, G. T. *Lord Lister, His Life and Work.* London: T. Fisher Unwin, 1913.

ARTICLES

"Meeting of the International Medical Congress." *Boston Medical and Surgical Journal* 95 (1876): 326–30.

"Letter From Philadelphia." *Boston Medical and Surgical Journal* 95 (1876): 363–69.

"The Antiseptic Method of Dressing Open Wounds, A Clinical Lecture by Prof. Joseph Lister, of Edinburgh, Delivered at Charity Hospital, New York, October 10, 1876." *Medical Record* 11 (1876): 695–96.

"Record of the Post-Mortem Examination of the Body of President J. A. Garfield, Made September 20, 1881, Commencing At 4:30 P.M., Eighteen Hours After Death, At Francklyn Cottage, Elberon, New Jersey." *American Journal of the Medical Sciences* 164 (1881): 583–90.

"Official Bulletins of the President's Case." *Boston Medical and Surgical Journal* 105 (1881): 299–312, 322–30.

Editorial. "President Garfield." *American Practitioner* 24 (1881): 113–15.

Editorial. "The President's Wound, and the Management of the Case." *Boston Medical and Surgical Journal* 105 (1881): 308–9.

Editorial. "The Death of the President." *Chicago Medical Journal and Examiner* 43 (1881): 426–27.

Editorial. "The President's Attendants." *Chicago Medical Review* 4 (1881): 385–86.

Editorial. "Medico-Legal Aspects of the President's Case." *Chicago Medical Review* 4 (1881): 409.

Editorial. "The President's Physicians." *Cincinnati Lancet and Clinic* 7 (1881): 63–64, 280–81.

Editorial. "The President." *Cincinnati Lancet and Clinic* 7 (1881): 107–8.

Editorial. "The President's Case." *Gaillard's Medical Journal* 32 (1881): 188–90, 277–82.

Editorial. "The Case of the Late President Garfield." *Lancet* 2 (1881): 553–54, 594, 723, 1097.

Editorial. "Reflections Upon the Case of President Garfield." *Medical Counselor* 6 (1881): 129–31.

Editorial. "The Case of President Garfield." *Medical Gazette* 8 (1881): 331.

Editorial. "The Case of President Garfield." *Medical News* 39 (1881): 631–35.

Editorial. "Notes on the President's Case." *Medical Record* 20 (1881): 295–96, 321–22.

Editorial. "The Death of Our Late President." *Medical and Surgical Reporter* 45 (1881): 383.

Editorial. "The Medical Jurisprudence of the Attempt to Assassinate the President." *New Orleans Medical and Surgical Journal* 9 (1881): 149–50.

Editorial. "The President's Case." *New Orleans Medical and Surgical Journal* 9 (1881): 231–32.

Editorial. "The Case of the Late President." *New York Medical Journal* 34 (1881): 489–94.

Editorial. "The Attack on the President." *Scribner's Monthly* 22 (1881): 784–85.

Editorial. "A Violation of Medical Ethics." *Walsh's Retrospect* 2 (1881): 457–59.

Editorial. "President Garfield's Wound and Its Treatment." *Walsh's Retrospect* 2 (1881): 623–33.

Editorial. "Professor Esmarch on Garfield's Wound." *Chicago Medical Review* 6 (1882): 409–10.

Editorial. "President Garfield's Case Again." *Medical News* 41 (1882): 128–30.

Editorial. "Professor Esmarch on the Case of President Garfield." *Medical News* 41 (1882): 294–95.

Editorial. "Our Dead President." *New York Medical Times* 9 (1882): 218–20.

Editorial. "Conflicting Opinions in the Case of the Late President." *Pacific Medical and Surgical Journal* 25 (1882): 231.

Editorial. "The Evidence." *Walsh's Retrospect* 3 (1882): 304–8.

Editorial. "Death of President McKinley." *Journal of the American Medical Association* 37 (1901): 779–84.

Agnew, D. Hayes. "Dr. Agnew on the Course and Location of the Bullet in the President's Body." *Medical Record* 20 (1881): 222–23.

Andrews, Edmund. "The Course of the Bullet in the President's Wound." *Chicago Medical Journal and Examiner* 43 (1881): 180–87.

———. "The Present State of Opinion on Antiseptic Surgery in the United States." *Chicago Medical Journal and Examiner* 44 (1882): 459–61.

Baker, Frank. "President Garfield's Case, A Diagnosis Made July 4th." *Walsh's Retrospect* 2 (1881): 617–22.

———. "President Garfield's Case Again." *Medical News* 41 (1882): 115–19.

Beckwith, S. R. "Dr. S. R. Beckwith's View." *New York Medical Times* 9 (1882): 221–22.

Bell, Alexander G. "Upon the Electrical Experiments to Determine the Location of the Bullet in the Body of the Late President Garfield: and Upon a Successful Form of Induction Balance for the Painless Detection of Metallic Masses in the Human Body." *American Journal of Science* 25 (1883): 26–61. (Also privately printed, Washington, D.C.: Gibson Brothers, 1882.)

Bliss, D. W. "Report of the Case of President Garfield, Accompanied with a Detailed Account of the Autopsy." *Medical Record* 20 (1881): 393–402.

———. "The Story of President Garfield's Illness, Told by the Physician in Charge." *Century Magazine* 23 (1881): 299–305.

———. "Feeding Per Rectum, As Illustrated in the Case of the Late President Garfield and Others." *Medical Record* 22 (1882): 64–69.

Boynton, S. "President Garfield's Case, Dr. Boynton's Statement." *American Observer Medical Monthly* 18 (1881): 492–94.

Brieger, Gert H. "American Surgery and the Germ Theory of Disease." *Bulletin of the History of Medicine* 40 (1966): 135–45.

———. "A Portrait of Surgery: Surgery in America, 1875–1889." *Surgical Clinics of North America* 67 (1987): 1181–1216.

Conant, R. W.: "Dr. Bliss' 'Greatest Triumph.'" *Medical Counselor* 6 (1881): 89–91.

Davis, James W. "Gunshot Wounds Which Caused the Deaths of Three of Our Presidents." *Military Surgeon* 77 (1935): 23–29.

Day, Richard H. "Review of the Surgical Treatment of President Garfield." *New Orleans Medical and Surgical Journal* 10 (1882): 81–95.

Deppisch, L. M. "Homeopathic Medicine and Presidential Health: Homeopathic Influences Upon Two Ohio Presidents." *Pharos* 60 (1997): 5–10.

Dukeman, W. H. "The President's Wound." *Medical Record* 20 (1881): 139.

Earle, A. Scott. "The Germ Theory in America: Antisepsis and Asepsis (1867–1900)." *Surgery* 65 (1969): 508–22.

Esmarch, Friedrich. "Concerning the Treatment of the Wound of President Garfield." *Boston Medical and Surgical Journal* 107 (1882): 234–37.

Figueira, M. "A Review of the Editorial on the Case of the Late President James A. Garfield." *Annals of Anatomy and Surgery* 4 (1881): 288–91.

Fish, Stewart A. "The Death of President Garfield." *Bulletin of the History of Medicine* 24 (1950): 378–97.

Gariepy, Thomas P. "The Introduction and Acceptance of Listerian Antisepsis in the United States." *Journal of the History of Medicine and Allied Sciences* 49 (1994): 167–206.

Gilchrist, J. G. "Why Did the President Die?" *Medical Counselor* 6 (1881): 33–38.

Girdner, John H. "Death of Garfield." *Munsey's Magazine* 26 (1902): 546–49.

Gorton, D. A. "Review of the 'Report On the Case of President Garfield.'" *New York Medical Times* 9 (1882): 235–36.

Hall, Courtney. "The Rise of Professional Surgery in the United States." *Bulletin of the History of Medicine* 26 (1952): 231–62.

Hamilton, Frank. H. "Dr. Hamilton on the Autopsy." *Boston Medical and Surgical Journal* 105 (1881): 311–12.

———. "The Case of President Garfield." *Gaillard's Medical Journal* 32 (1881): 234–44.

———. "The Case of President Garfield." *Medical Gazette* 8 (1881): 333–34.

———. "Dr. Hamilton's Bill for Professional Services to President Garfield." *Medical News* 41 (1882): 585–86.

Hammond, William A. "The Condition of the Arteries After Death." *Medical Record* 20 (1881): 668–69.

Hammond, William A., J. Marion Sims, John Ashhurst, and John T. Hodgen. "The Surgical Treatment of President Garfield." *North American Review* 133 (1881): 578–610.

Harper, S. B. "Gunshot Wounds of Three Presidents of the United States."
    Proceedings of the Staff Meetings of the Mayo Clinic 19 (1944): 11–19.
Hunt, William. "Correspondence." *Medical News* 39 (1881): 699–704.
    (See also *Boston Medical and Surgical Journal* 105 (1881): 505–7.)
———. "The Post-Mortem Examination of President Garfield." *Medical
    Record* 20 (1881): 642.
Jennings, R. S. "Cooling Apparatus Used at the White House." *Boston
    Medical and Surgical Journal* 105 (1881): 470–71.
Kelly, Howard A. "Was the Thoracic Duct Injured in the Case of
    President Garfield?" *Medical News* 40 (1882): 30.
King, G. W. "The Victim of His Physicians, A Professional Review of the
    Case of President James A. Garfield." *American Medical Journal* 30
    (1902): 219–30.
Miller, Joseph M. "The Death of James Abram Garfield." *Surgery,
    Gynecology, & Obstetrics* 107 (1958): 113–18.
Parker, Owen W. "The Assassination and Gunshot Wound of President
    James A. Garfield." *Minnesota Medicine* 34 (1951): 227–33, 258.
Pilcher, Lewis S. Editorial, "The Case of the Late President James A.
    Garfield." *Annals of Anatomy and Surgery* 4 (1881): 219–27.
———. Editorial, "Editorial Rejoinder." *Annals of Anatomy and Surgery* 4
    (1881): 291–94.
Prichard, Robert W., and A. L. Herring. "The Problem of the President's
    Bullet." *Surgery, Gynecology, & Obstetrics* 92 (1951): 625–33.
Reyburn, Robert. "Clinical History of the Case of President James
    Abram Garfield." *Journal of the American Medical Association* 22
    (1894): 411–17, 460–64, 498–502, 545–49, 578–82, 621–24,
    664–69.
———. "The Case of President James A. Garfield: An Abstract of the
    Clinical History." *American Medicine* 2 (1901): 498–501.
Richmond, Phyllis A. "American Attitudes Toward the Germ Theory of
    Disease (1860–1880)." *Journal of the History of Medicine and Allied
    Sciences* 9 (1954): 428–54.
Rockwell, C. A. "From Mentor to Elberon." *Century Magazine* 23
    (1882): 431–38.
Roos, Charles A. "Physicians to the Presidents, and Their Patients: A
    Bibliography." *Bulletin of the Medical Library Association* 49 (1961):
    291–360.
Rutkow, Ira M. "Edwin Hartley Pratt and Orificial Surgery: Unorthodox
    Surgical Practice in Nineteenth-Century United States. *Surgery* 114
    (1993): 558–63.
———. "William Tod Helmuth and Andrew Jackson Howe: Surgical
    Sectariansim in 19th-Century America." *Archives of Surgery* 129
    (1994): 662–68.

Rutkow, Lainie W., and Ira M. Rutkow. "Homeopaths, Surgery, and the
    Civil War; Edward C. Franklin and the Struggle to Achieve Medical
    Pluralism in the Union Army." *Archives of Surgery* 139 (2004):
    785–91.
Schuppert, M. "A Review of the Wound, Treatment, and Death of James
    A. Garfield, Late President of The United States of America."
    Gaillard's Medical Journal 32 (1881): 494–517.
Shrady, George F. "Antiseptic Surgery," editorial. *Medical Record* 15
    (1879): 206–8.
———. "The Wounded President," editorial. *Medical Record* 20 (1881):
    42–44.
———. "The President's Wound," editorial. *Medical Record* 20 (1881):
    71–72.
———. "The President's Progress," editorial, *Medical Record* 20 (1881):
    154–55.
———. "The President's Progress," editorial. *Medical Record* 20 (1881):
    186.
———. "President Garfield," editorial. *Medical Record* 20 (1881): 199.
———. "President Garfield," editorial. *Medical Record* 20 (1881): 226.
———. "The End at Last," editorial. *Medical Record* 20 (1881):
    350–51.
———. "Surgical and Pathological Reflections on President Garfield's
    Wound," editorial. *Medical Record* 20 (1881): 404–6.
———. "The Late President Garfield's Case," editorial. *Medical Record*
    20 (1881): 410–11.
———. "Professional Fees in the Late President's Case," editorial.
    Medical Record 20 (1881): 574–75.
———. "The Question of Malpractice in the Case of the Late President
    Garfield," editorial. *Medical Record* 20 (1881): 600–601.
Sigerist, Henry E. "Surgery at the Time of the Introduction of
    Antisepsis." *Journal of the Missouri State Medical Association* 32
    (1935): 169–76.
Smith, Andrew H. "Can We Diagnosticate Obliteration of the
    Receptaculum Chyli?" *Medical Record* 54 (1899): 813–15.
———. "President Garfield at Elberon." *American Medicine* 9 (1905):
    118–20.
Stevens, Ralph. "A President's Assassination." *Journal of the American
    Medical Association* 246 (1981): 1673–74.
Stow, T. Dwight. "Treatment of President Garfield." *Homoeopathic
    Physician* 1 (1881): 533–38.
Temkin, Owsei, and Janet Koudelka. "Simon Newcomb and the
    Location of President Garfield's Bullet." *Bulletin of the History of
    Medicine* 24 (1950): 393–97.

Tindall, William. "Echoes of a Surgical Tragedy." *Records of the Columbia Historical Society* 23 (1920): 147–66.

Turnipseed, E. B. "A Dissenting Voice from the Standpoints Taken by D. W. Bliss, M.D., In Regard to the Diagnosis, Prognosis, and Treatment of the Case of President Garfield." *Medical Record* 20 (1881): 621–24.

Vincent, Esther H. "Presidential Gunshot Wounds, Three Case Reports." *Surgery, Gynecology, & Obstetrics* 91 (1950): 115–19.

Warren, J. Collins. "Case of President Garfield, Statement of Dr. J. Collins Warren." *Boston Medical and Surgical Journal* 105 (1881): 463–66.

Watson, B. A. "Lister's System of Aseptic Wound-Treatment Versus Its Modifications." *Transactions of the American Surgical Association* 1 (1883): 205–23.

Weiner, Bradley K. "The Case of James A. Garfield, A Historical Perspective." *Spine* 28 (2003): E183–E186.

Weir, Robert F. "On the Antiseptic Treatment of Wounds, and Its Results." *New York Medical Journal* 26 (1877): 561–80; and 26 (1878): 31–51.

Weisse, Faneuil D. "Surgical Reflections and Anatomical Observations." *Medical Record* 20 (1881): 57–61.

———. "Surgico-Anatomical Study of the Gunshot Wound of President Garfield." *Medical Record* 20 (1881): 402–3.

White, J. William. "President Garfield's Case." *Medical News* 41 (1882): 247–48.

———. "A Review of Some of the More Important Surgical Problems of President Garfield's Case." *Medical News* 40 (1882): 677–83.

Wilcox, Howard G. "The President Ails: American Medicine in Retrospect." *Delaware Medical Journal* 53 (1981): 201–10.

Young, D. S. "Diagnosis of the Gun-Shot Wound of President Garfield." *Cincinnati Lancet and Clinic* 7 (1881): 369–72.

Acknowledgments

Few histories stand alone, and I received inspiration and guidance from numerous earlier works on Garfield, particularly Harry J. Brown and Frederick D. Williams's *The Diary of James A. Garfield;* Robert Caldwell's *James A. Garfield, Party Chieftain;* Margaret Leech and Harry J. Brown's *The Garfield Orbit: The Life of President James A. Garfield;* Allan Peskin's *Garfield, A Biography;* John C. Ridpath's *The Life and Work of James A. Garfield;* Theodore C. Smith's *The Life and Letters of James Abram Garfield;* and John M. Taylor's *Garfield of Ohio, The Available Man.* I must also thank the library and research staffs at the New York Academy of Medicine and the New York Public Library for their assistance.

This book was originally intended as a behind-the-scenes story of the medical aspects of Garfield's assassination. Arthur M. Schlesinger, Jr., wisely proposed that the work be expanded into a political biography. I thank him for his suggestion and the opportunity to participate in the American Presidents series. To my editor, Paul Golob, I offer sincere thanks for his professional and scholarly skills. Eric Simonoff, my agent at Janklow and Nesbit Associates, is extraordinary and finds writing projects I never thought possible.

Finally, to my parents, Bea and Al Rutkow, this book further validates your many sacrifices made to ensure that I received a superb education. To my wife, Beth, and our children, Lainie and Eric, I dedicate this book. Lainie, a lawyer and fierce protector of the public's health, is an amazing woman who lights up everyone's life. Eric, a lawyer who advocates for human rights in international development, provides sincerity to all who know him. Beth is the love of my life and without her patience and sustenance I would accomplish little.

Index

ABOUT THE AUTHOR

Ira Rutkow is a clinical professor of surgery at the University of Medicine and Dentistry of New Jersey. He also holds a doctorate of public health from Johns Hopkins University. He is the author of *Bleeding Blue and Gray: Civil War Surgery and the Evolution of American Medicine* and *Surgery: An Illustrated History*, which was a *New York Times* Notable Book of the Year. He and his wife divide their time between New York City and the Catskills.